DISCLAIMER

CW00516696

Contents

INTRODUCTION

Amigurumi Zoo: Crochet Adorable Animal Friends invites you to enter its wonderful world. Let your imagination go wild as you learn to crochet cute little creatures. This book will teach you how to draw your favorite animals, from their wacky tails and expressive ears to their detailed face expressions. Learn the trick to choosing yarn colors and textures that reflect each animal's personality. You'll learn the skills necessary to construct and customize a gorgeous menagerie from adorable patterns with the help of knowledgeable guides. Discover the many uses of Amigurumi, from decorative accents to presents to imaginative games. This book will help crocheters of all skill levels create a menagerie of adorable, cuddly pets. Prepare to sew together cherished recollections.

Chapter 1

INTRODUCTION TO AMIGURUMI AND CROCHET BASICS

1. An overview of what Amigurumi is and its popularity

If you appreciate handcrafted goods, you've probably heard of Amigurumi. Even among those who like handcrafted goods, the concept of Amigurumi can be readily misconstrued because of its relative unfamiliarity.

Those of you familiar with the cherry blossom culture know that the word "amigurumi" has its roots in Japan. The Japanese crocheting technique of amigurumi has gained international renown. People find out more about Amigurumi because the plush animals it produces can be used to make thoughtful and endearing presents.

The word "amigurumi" comes from the Japanese words for "crochet" and "stuffed doll," respectively. The term "Amigurumi" has come to mean knitted or crocheted toys.

Amigurumi, the crocheted stuffed toys, were created in Japan. Beautiful knitted and crocheted animals and other items are the end results of this craft.

Creativity, inventiveness, and the kind of attention to detail typical of youngsters are essential for successful amigurumi projects. Making soft, attractive, and exquisite Amigurumi plush animals calls for a lot of effort.

Amigurumi may have originated in Japan, but its adorable designs, painstaking attention to detail, and profound symbolic value have made it a global phenomenon. Amigurumi's rising popularity isn't slowing down any time soon.

1.1 What is handmade Amigurumi used for?

Amigurumi items, like the cuddly stuffed toys made from yarn weaving, are made for decoration and to serve as a very special accent.

Put to use as a hook

Amigurumi is most often used to create hangers. It's perfect for crafting whatever you'd like, from key chains to phone holders to backpack straps. The cute plush animals are not only adorable, but also a conversation starter when attached to a keychain, phone, backpack, etc.

Knitting also results in extremely one-of-a-kind embellishments, such as hooks. Each amigurumi item appears to be one-of-a-kind because it is crocheted by hand and relies on the individual's imagination and crocheting skills.

Make use of as a table centerpiece

The versatility of larger crochet stuffed animals as decorative accents is exceptional. The knitted knitted teddy bears can be used to decorate the table, the living room, and the window frame.

You'll feel better just looking at the bright and cuddly Amigurumi teddy bears.

Toy manufacturing

Amigurumi will be a great friend for kids because they love teddy animals. The knitted teddy bears will be cuddly, beautiful, and brightly colored; they will also be just the right size for children to play with.

More regulation is needed for the use of Amigurumi bears as baby toys. To ensure the baby's safety, greater standards are also needed for product quality.

Give an Amigurumi as a present.

The use of Amigurumi teddy bears as presents is deeply sentimental. Because of the time, care, and attention to detail required to make these goods, the intended receiver must be of the utmost importance.

Moreover, the recipient of an Amigurumi present aids in making that person feel truly valued. Thus, this present has both monetary and emotional worth, strengthening the bond between the giver and the recipient.

1.2 Exceptional benefits of the teddy bear Amigurumi

This is the pinnacle of imagination.

It takes a lot of imagination, shaping skill, and the ability to harmonize eye colors to make an Amigurumi teddy bear. Those that are able to stick with it undoubtedly flourish in their ability to think outside the box.

Form with such beauty and grace

Finished works of Amigurumi art demand the attention to detail and boundless creativity of children. As a result, most product designs are quite pleasant to look at. This is why the product is primarily employed in the ornamental industry.

Artwork that is one of a kind since it was handcrafted

Amigurumi is a type of knitting or crocheting that creates one-of-a-kind, adorable toys. This hobby is popular among both the young and the middle-aged.

Easy to locate and inexpensive ingredients

Because they are handmade, most amigurumi bears are made from wool. An inexpensive and simple-to-obtain component. However the Amigurumi bear product is immensely popular because it combines great aesthetics with deep personal significance when crocheted by hand

How to Make an Amigurumi Bear

Creating a real Amigurumi bear is not easy, it is a process that requires meticulousness and patience. That's why Amigurumi is called an art, and becoming an artist takes a lot of practice.

Prepare the model

The first thing in creating an Amigurumi bear is the model. An Amigurumi bear is created from thousands of crochet stitches, and when you first start with this art, you will not be able to determine how many stitches to create the desired shape. And these models will be templates for you to create shapes easily through crochet stitches.

A typical model for beginners in this art will fully describe what you need to do. The model will show the full number of crochet stitches, the type of crochet you need to make in each round.

The model is also extremely diverse from basic to advanced so you can practice from easy to difficult. Advanced patterns require more complex knitting techniques.

2. Prepare materials to make Amigurumi

After settling on a pattern, the next step in making Amigurumi goods is to choose the appropriate yarn and needles. The necessary supplies are:

Wool:

When making an Amigurumi, you can use just about any kind of yarn you like. If you want the best results, though, stick to the creator's recommended type selections.

No matter what kind of wool you're looking for, it's important to consider the yarn's thickness and fineness. If the pattern doesn't specify yarn type or thickness, standard cotton and wool yarns are safe bets.

Hook Needle:

This is an indispensable tool in the art of crocheting in general and Amigurumi in particular. The size of crochet needles used in Amigurumi is usually between 2mm - 5mm, and you must choose the right type for the size of the wool you use.

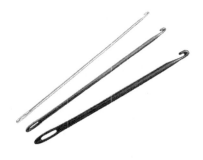

Stuffing cotton:

Knit the crochet to create the shape, but to bring the Amigurumi to life you need to stuff them. There are many cotton materials to stuff Amigurumi, but Polyester is the most popular.

This material can be easily found at stores selling handmade accessories or handicrafts.

Wool sewing needles:

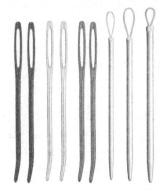

The Amigurumi craft involves crocheting individual components and sewing them back together with a woolen needle. To complete your Amigurumi bear, all you need is an old embroidery needle with a round needle tip.

Crochet stitches used in Amigurumi

There is a vast range of crochet stitches used in Amigurumi, each of which is best suited to a specific pattern. More intricate crochet stitches are required for more difficult patterns.

Magic ring: This is considered the basic crochet stitch and is used by almost any crochet bear. Magic ring is a small circle, the stitches are hooked together.

Single Crochet / X Stitch (Sc or Single Crochet): This is the most used crochet stitch.

Increase/V stitch (Inc or Single Crochet Increase). You will have to crochet 2 single stitches on the same leg of the previous loop, which will increase the total stitches of the current loop compared to the previous loop.

Reduced Stitch / Stitch A (Dec): With this stitch, you will hook 2 stitches into 1 stitch. Thus, this type of crochet will reduce the total stitches of the current loop compared to the previous loop. You should also use the invisibility reduction nose to make the bear more beautiful.

Slip stitch (ss or slip stitch): Usually a slip stitch is used to finish crocheting a certain part of the bear.

Everyone seems to be drawn to amigurumi, the Japanese craft of making woolen toys through knitting and crocheting. It's one of a kind and stunning, so it works great as a showpiece or as a present that the recipient will treasure forever. Everyone wishes they could learn this fascinating art of amigurumi.

CHAPTER 2:
GETTING STARTED WITH ANIMAL AMIGURUMI

1. Selecting yarn colors and textures for different animals.

Currently on the market there are many types of wool yarn on the market with enough quality, size, rich price, because that's why when you first start, you will not be overwhelmed right! Each type of wool yarn has different materials and textures, we can freely choose depending on the preferences and aesthetic taste of each person, to use for crocheting woolen animals (must be stuffed inside), it is important. The best thing you need to keep in mind is to choose a lens that is NOT stretchy, because if the yarn is elastic, it will distort the shape of the animal when crocheted or stuffed, revealing the cotton inside, etc.

Each wool roll has a label with detailed information about the wool's material, thickness, recommended needle size, etc., as well as the wool's brand, color code, and country of origin.

- Yarn Weight
Yarn weight refers to the thickness of the yarn and is divided into 7 different categories, from lace (0) to jumbo (7).

The most common yarn weights for amigurumi are in the middle of the range – DK (type 3) or coarse wool weights (type 4).

These medium-weight yarns are easy to work with and produce strong fabrics that hold their shape well.

As a general rule, thinner yarn will produce smaller, more detailed amigurumi. However, they can be more difficult to work with, especially for beginners. On the other hand, thicker yarns that are bulky and super bulky (types 5 and 6) will make for a super snug and full amigurumi toy.

- **Definition and structure of stitches** The next factor to consider is the seam definition of the yarn. We have found that fine yarns with consistent twist give the best results. No frills, no ruffles, just clean, clear lines. And while the cotton threads may look cute (hello, teddy bears!), their matte texture makes it hard to see your stitches and keep track of your loops. These yarns are more difficult to work with and are best reserved for those with some experience. Mostly, you should look for yarns that are sturdy and not too stretchy. This will help your amigurumi project stay in shape.

- **Durability**
Yarn strength is key and it is important to choose yarns that are easy to care for and will last over time. Especially when making children's crafts, you'll want a yarn that can withstand multiple hugs and hugs without clumping or ruffled hair. Also, look for machine washable yarns for those inevitable cleanup situations.

- **Color Options**
Finally, look for yarns with a wide range of colors so you can find the perfect color for your project. And if you're going to be making dolls, 14

you'll also want to look for yarns that come in various skin tones, such as Lion Brand Skein Tones.

Furthermore, attention should be paid to the consistency of the dye batch. Good dye lot uniformity means that the color is the same from batch to batch of yarn. This is important if you are using more than one skein of yarn for your project or if you are doing several amigurumi projects with the same yarn and want them to match.

- Fiber content

Now, about the fiber content. The fiber content of the yarn affects how easy it is to care for your finished project as well as its softness, durability, cost and ease of work.

The most common yarns for amigurumi are acrylic and cotton, although sometimes chenille and blanket yarn are also good choices.

Acrylic: Acrylic yarn is an inexpensive option that comes in a variety of colors.

This yarn is accessible and good for beginners. Plus, it's machine washable! But be aware, acrylic fibers tend to clump and become lint after many uses, so this may not be the best choice for toys that will be hugged by many children.

Cotton: Cotton yarn is very durable and easy to wash, so it will last well over time and many times of use. Cotton has excellent seam definition and tends to be much less lumpy than acrylic fibers. Cotton doesn't have many downsides, but it can be stiffer when working. If you find "kitchen cotton" yarn too rough on your hands, try using soft, smooth, polished cotton yarn instead.

Chenille yarn and quilt: Finally, chenille yarn and quilt can be good choices for some amigurumi projects. These fibers are super soft and are ideal for giant stuffed animals and cuddly toys.

2. Best Yarn For Amigurumi:

* 2.1 Best Cotton Yarns

Lion Brand 24/7 Cotton – This worsted weight is made of 100% mercerized cotton. It's machine washable and dryable, with excellent durability and stitch definition. It doesn't split easily and is available in a wide variety of colors.

Schachenmayr Catania – This lightweight, sport yarn is great for making smaller stitches and more detailed amigurumi patterns. It's made of 100% combed and mercerized cotton. This option is machine washable but not machine dryable. In addition, washing it in hotter water the first time is recommended to prevent the color from bleeding.

Paintbox Yarns Cotton DK – This DK-weight yarn is soft, easy to work with, and made of 100% cotton. It's available in tons of color options, so it's a great choice if you need a specific shade for a doll or a toy animal.

WeCrochet Dishie – This cotton option is super durable and ideal for making an amigurumi project that lasts many years. It's machine washable, soft, and holds its color well. This worsted-weight yarn comes in solid colors as well as multi and twist options.

LION BRAND 24/7 COTTON

PAINTBOX YARNS
COTTON DK

SCHACHENMAYR CATANIA

WECROCHET DISHIE

2.2 Best Acrylic Yarns

Joann Big Twist – Made by Joann Fabrics, Big Twist is an affordable and durable 100% acrylic yarn. It's also machine washable. The downsides of Big Twist are that the dye lots are not guaranteed, and some crafters find that it splits and pills more easily than other yarns.

Lion Brand Basic Stitch & Skein Tones – Available in many shades, Lion Brand Basic Stitch is a great option. In particular, the Skein Tones range is some of the best yarn for making lifelike amigurumi dolls. It's a 100% acrylic, worsted-weight yarn that's soft, easy to work with, and doesn't pill easily.

Yarn Art Jeans – Yarn Art Jeans is a 55% cotton, 45% polyacrylic yarn that's smooth and soft. It's a sport-weight yarn that's great for smaller or more detailed amigurumi projects.

Paintbox Yarns Simply DK – This 100% acrylic, DK-weight yarn is available in a wide range of color options – from pastels to bright colors to muted tones. It's easy to work with and a cost-effective option for making amigurumi.

YARN ART JEANS

JOANN BIG TWIST

LION BRAND BASIC STITCH & SKEIN TONES

PAINTBOX YARNS SIMPLY DK

2.3 Best Specialty Yarns

Bernat Blanket – This yarn is a 100% polyester, super bulky option that's ideal for making larger amigurumi projects. It would make a great choice for a teddy bear or any larger, fluffy, lovable friend! It's a chenille-style yarn that's available in both solid and multi colors.

Paintbox Yarns Chenille – This super soft and cozy choice from Paintbox Yarns is 100% polyester. It's a bulky yarn that works up quickly and is machine washable. This option is one of the best chenille yarns for amigurumi. It's ideal for larger projects or amigurumi you're making for a baby or child.

KnitPicks Fable Fur – Fable Fur is a super bulky, faux fur yarn made from a premium polyester that doesn't shrink and holds its shape well. This yarn works up quickly, and the faux fur makes it extra soft and snuggly. However, the texture also makes it more challenging to see your stitches. Plus, it needs to be hand washed.

Woobles Easy Peasy Yarn – This yarn has a super smooth texture and clear stitch definition. It doesn't snag, fray, or split easily, making it easy to work with and one of the best yarn options for beginners. It's a worsted-weight yarn made of 75% cotton and 25% nylon. It's machine washable and is available in 13 colors.

BERNAT BLANKET

WOOBLES EASY PEASY YARN

PAINTBOX YARNS CHENILLE

KNITPICKS FABLE FUR

3. THE BEST HOOK SIZES FOR AMIGURUMI

Using the hook size specified for the yarn on the label can result in sloppy stitches and excess stuffing showing through while making an amigurumi. That's because amigurumi hooks must be smaller than the yarn manufacturer's suggested hook size. This amigurumi hook size chart will remove all doubt from your selection process.

The difference between using a hook that is too tiny and too large for your yarn is negligible. Crocheting with a hook that is too small will tire your hands out quickly as you try to force the hook through the stitch. But if it's too huge, your amigurumi will have holes and appear unprofessional.

Listen up if you've been told that making amigurumi requires you to crochet more tightly and with more tension. Tight, hole-free stitches should be the result of nothing more than using the correct hook size. You won't have to adjust your technique as long as you're using the right size hook for your amigurumi.

It's also worth noting that even within the categories of yarn weight, there is a great deal of diversity. Even among similar yarns, variations in thickness and elasticity can be found. You'll find a variety of recommended hook sizes and yarns for each category in the chart below.

AMIGURUMI HOOK SIZE & YARN WEIGHT

YARN WEIGHT SYMBOL & CATEGORY NAME	TYPES OF YARN IN THIS CATEGORY	TYPICALLY RECOMMENDED HOOK IN METRIC SIZE (MM)	RECOMMENDED AMIGURUMI HOOK IN METRIC SIZE (MM)
0 LACE	• Fingering • Thread • 1-3 ply	1.4 – 2.25 MM	0.6 – 1.25 MM
1 SUPER FINE	• Sock • Fingering • Baby • 4 ply	2.25 – 3.5 MM	1.25 – 1.5 MM
2 FINE	• Sport • Baby • 5 ply	3.5 – 4.5 MM	1.75 – 2.25 MM
3 LIGHT	• DK • Light worsted • 8 ply	4.5 – 5.5 MM	2.25 – 2.75 MM
4 MEDIUM	• Worsted • Aran • Afghan • 10-12 ply	5.5 – 6.5 MM	2.75 – 3.75 MM
5 BULKY	• Chunky • Craft • Rug • 12-14 ply	6.5 – 9 MM	4 – 5 MM
6 SUPER BULKY	• Super Bulky • Super Chunky • Roving • 14-16 ply	9 – 15 MM	6.5 – 9 MM
7 JUMBO	• Jumbo • Roving • 16 ply+	15 MM AND LARGER	10 MM AND LARGER

A HANDY TRICK TO FINDING THE RIGHT HOOK SIZE

If you use the more common yarn sizes (levels 2-5), a handy trick for figuring out what hook size to use is to take the smallest recommended hook size and subtract 2 mm to get the amigurumi hook size you should use.

Lightweight (dk or light-worsted) yarn calls for a hook size of 4.5 to 5.5 mm, as an example. Subtract 2 millimeters from the smallest suggested hook size (4.5 mm). Therefore, a 2.5 mm hook is ideal for amigurumi projects. In the United States, a crochet hook size of 2.5 mm is not particularly common, but it falls between the more usual sizes of size B (2.25 mm) and size C (2.75 mm).

RESIZING AN AMIGURUMI PATTERN

If you want to get extreme with your amigurumi, you'll love micro crochet! For micro amigurumi, you use fine thread and a thin crochet hook to make amigurumi that can sit on your finger tips! You can go as tiny as possible by using cotton sewing thread and a 0.6 mm hook (although this is NOT for the faint of heart).

CHAPTER 3:
BRINGING ANIMAL AMIGURUMI TO LIFE

CAT

The first step is to crochet the ears. Next you'll crochet the head, and the ears will be crocheted in as you go. Then you'll crochet all the limbs and tail, and those will be attached as you crochet the body.

This cat crochet pattern is great for beginners

This cat crochet pattern is great for beginners

As long as you know the basic stitches of amigurumi (single crochet, increase and invisible decrease), you should be able to complete this pattern easy-peasy.

Recommended Sequence

Here are the steps to create your cat, in order:

- Crochet the Ears
- Crochet the Head
- Crochet the Legs
- Crochet the Tail
- Crochet the Arms
- Crochet the Body
- Attach the Head to the Body
- Embroider the Nose
- Add Whiskers

23

Supplies
- 3.5mm (E) hook
- 15mm safety eyes
- Stitch markers
- Yarn needle
- Fiber fill
- Disappearing ink marker
- Fishing line

- **Yarn (acrylic, weight 4) – 235 total yards**
- White – 59 yards (I used Red Heart Super Saver – White)
- Pink – 4 yards (I used Red Heart Soft Yarn – Rose Blush)
- Light Gray – 143 yards (I used Red Heart Soft Yarn – Light Grey Heather)
- Dark Gray – 29 yards (I used Red Heart Super Saver – Charcoal)

Notes
- Abbreviations
- ch – chain
- sc – single crochet
- inc – complete two single crochets within the same stitch
- dec – combine two stitches into one with an invisible decrease
- *sc x* – repeat the instructions between asterisks(*) the indicated number of times.
- {P+LG} – color-change increase: complete two single crochets within the same stitch. The first single crochet should be in pink, and the second single crochet should be in light gray.
- (sc x) – attach a body part while completing the stitches inside parentheses as instructed by the pattern.

* Ears (make 2)
LG = Light Gray | P = Pink

- 01. LG: start 6 sc into a magic ring [6]
- 02. *sc, inc* 3 times [9]
- 03. sc, P: inc, LG: *sc 2, inc* 2 times, sc [12]
- 04. sc, P: sc 2, color-change increase: {P+LG}, LG: *sc 3, inc* 2 times [15]
- 05. sc, P: sc 4, LG: sc 10 [15]
- 06. sc, P: sc, inc, sc 2, LG: sc 2, inc, sc 4, inc, sc 2 [18]
- 07. sc, P: sc 6, LG: sc 11 [18]
- 08. sc, P: sc 6, LG: sc 11 [18]
- 09. sc, P: sc 7, LG: inc, sc 8, inc [20]
- 10. sc, P: sc 7, LG: sc 12 [20]

Fasten off and leave a 18" tail. Do not stuff. Pinch the final round together and slip stitch closed. Hide the tail inside the work. Each ear will be attached while crocheting the head at a later step.

* Head

- W = White | LG = Light Gray | DG = Dark Gray

- 01. W: Chain 3 Start: ch 3, inc in 2nd ch from hook, 5sc in the last ch. Continue on the other side of the chain base, 3sc in the last ch [10]
- 02. inc, sc 2, *inc* 3 times, sc 2, *inc* 2 times [16]
- 03. inc, sc 4, *inc* 2 times, sc, inc, sc 4, *inc* 2 times, sc [22]
- 04. inc, sc 6, *inc, sc* 2 times, inc, sc 6, *inc, sc* 2 times [28]
- 05. sc 11, inc, sc 15, inc [30]
- 06 – 07. sc in each st around [30]

25

- 08. *sc 3, dec* 4 times, sc 2, LG: sc, dec, sc 3, dec [24]
- 09. *sc, inc* 12 times [36]
- 10. *sc 5, inc* 6 times [42]
- 11. sc 3, inc, *sc 6, inc* 5 times, sc 3 [48]
- 12. *sc 7, inc* 6 times [54]

Marking Stitches for the Eyes: Insert two markers 18 stitches apart between rounds 11 & 12. These markers will show you where to place your safety eyes at a later step.

- 13. sc 4, inc, *sc 8, inc* 5 times, sc 4 [60]
- 14. sc 10, DG: sc 7, LG: 43 [60]
- 15. sc in each st around [60]
- 16. sc 59, DG: sc [60]
- 17. sc 5, LG: sc 3, DG: sc 12, LG: sc 3, DG: sc 6, LG: sc 31 [60]
- 18. sc in each st around [60]

Attaching the Ears: In round 19, the parentheses indicate where you should attach each ear.

- 19. sc, Attach the first ear: (sc 10), sc 7, Attach the second ear: (sc 10), sc 32 [60]

At the end of round 19, the ears should be centered above the snout. If your ears appear off center, redo the round and adjust the placement of the ears as necessary.

- 20. sc 12, DG: sc 5, LG: sc 43 [60]
- 21 – 22. sc in each st around [60]
- 23. sc 7, DG: sc 17, LG: sc 36 [60]
- 24. sc 4, dec, *sc 8, dec* 5 times, sc 4 [54]
- 25. *sc 7, dec* 6 times [48]

- 26. sc 3, dec, *sc 6, dec* 5 times, sc 3 [42]
- 27. *sc 5, dec* 6 times [36]
- 28. sc 2, dec, *sc 4, dec* 5 times, sc 2 [30]

Stuff head ¾ full and create indents for the eyes. Insert your safety eyes and secure the backings.

- 29. *sc 3, dec* 6 times [24]
- 30. sc, dec, *sc 2, dec* 5 times, sc [18]
- 31. *sc, dec* 6 times [12]

Finish stuffing.

- 32. *dec* 6 times [6]

Cut working yarn and close with an ultimate finish.

* Legs (make 2)

W = White | LG = Light Gray | DG = Dark Gray

- 01. W: Chain 3 Start: ch 3, inc in 2nd ch from hook, 5sc in the last ch. Continue on the other side of the chain base, 3sc in the last ch [10]
- 02. inc, sc 2, *inc* 3 times, sc 2, *inc* 2 times [16]
- 03. inc, sc 4, *inc* 2 times, sc, inc, sc 4, *inc* 2 times, sc [22]
- 04. inc, sc 6, *inc, sc* 2 times, inc, sc 6, *inc, sc* 2 times [28]
- 05. inc, sc 8, inc, sc 2, inc, sc, inc, sc 8, inc, sc 2, inc, sc [34]

- 06 – 07. sc in each st around [34]
- 08. sc 28, *dec* 3 times [31]
- 09. *dec* 3 times, sc 21, *dec* 2 times [26]
- 10. *dec* 2 times, sc 22 [24]
- 11. sc 12, LG: sc 12 [24]
- 12. sc 17, dec, sc 5 [23]
- 13. sc 12, DG: sc 11 [23]
- 14. sc 12, LG: sc 9, dec [22]
- 15. sc in each st around [22]
- 16. sc 10, dec, sc, DG: sc 9 [21]
- 17. sc 12, LG: sc 9 [21]
- 18. sc 19, dec [20]
- 19. sc 13, DG: sc 7 [20]
- 20. sc 9, dec, sc 2, LG: sc 7 [19]
- 21. sc 17, dec [18]
- 22. *sc 7, dec* 2 times [16]
- 23. *sc 2, dec* 4 times [12]

Fasten off and leave a 18″ tail. Stuff the leg. Pinch the final round together and slip stitch closed, then hide the tail inside the work. Each leg will be attached while crocheting the body at a later step.

* Tail

W = White | LG = Light Gray | DG = Dark Gray

01. W: start 6 sc into a magic ring [6]
02. inc in each st around [12]
03 – 05. sc in each st around [12]
06. LG: sc in each st around [12]
*07. dec, sc 3, *inc* 2 times, sc 3, dec [12]*

28

- 08. DG: dec, sc 3, *inc* 2 times, sc 3, dec [12]
- 09. LG: dec, sc 3, *inc* 2 times, sc 3, dec [12]
- 10. dec, sc 3, *inc* 2 times, sc 3, dec [12]
- 11. DG: dec, sc 3, *inc* 2 times, sc 3, dec [12]
- 12 -13. LG: sc in each st around [12]
- 14. sc, DG: sc 11 [12]
- 15. sc, LG: sc 11 [12]
- 16. sc in each st around [12]
- 17. sc 2, DG: sc 10 [12]
- 18. sc 2, LG: sc 10 [12]
- 19. dec, sc 8, dec [10]

Fasten off and leave a 18″ yarn tail. Stuff the the tail. Pinch the final round together and slip stitch closed, then hide the yarn tail inside the work. The tail will be attached while crocheting the body at a later step.

* Arms (make 2)

W = White | LG = Light Gray | DG = Dark Gray
- 01. W: start 6 sc into a magic ring [6]
- 02. inc in each st around [12]
- 03. *sc, inc* 6 times [18]
- 04. sc, inc, *sc 2, inc* 5 times, sc [24]
- 05 – 06. sc in each st around [24]
- 07. sc 2, dec, sc 16, dec, sc 2 [22]
- 08. sc, dec, sc 16, dec, sc [20]
- 09. sc 12, LG: sc 8 [20]
- 10. sc 9, dec, sc 9 [19]
- 11. sc 11, DG: sc 8 [19]
- 12. sc 11, LG: sc 6, dec [18]
- 13. sc in each st around [18]

- 14. sc 8, dec, sc 2, DG: sc 6 [17]
- 15. sc 11, LG: sc 6 [17]
- 16. sc 15, dec [16]
- 17. sc 11, DG: sc 5 [16]
- 18. sc 7, dec, sc 2, LG: sc 5 [15]
- 19. sc in each st around [15]
- 20. sc 11, DG: sc 2, dec [14]
- 21. sc 11, LG: sc 3 [14]
- 22. sc 6, dec, sc 6 [13]
- 23. sc 11, DG: sc 2 [13]
- 24. sc 11, LG: dec [12]
- 25 – 26. sc in each st around [12]

Fasten off and leave a 18″ tail. Stuff the arm. Pinch the final round together and slip stitch closed, then hide the tail inside the work. Each arm will be attached while crocheting the body at a later step

* Body

- W = White | LG = Light Gray | DG = Dark Gray

- 01. LG: start 6 sc into a magic ring [6]
- 02. inc in each st around [12]
- 03. *sc, inc* 6 times [18]
- 04. sc, inc, *sc 2, inc* 5 times, sc [24]
- 05. *sc 3, inc* 6 times [30]
- 06. sc 2, inc, *sc 4, inc* 5 times, sc 2 [36]

Attaching the Legs: Attach the legs where instructed while crocheting the next round.

- 07. Attach the first leg in the next six stitches: (sc 5, inc), sc 5, inc, Attach the second leg in the next six stitches: (sc 5, inc), *sc 5, inc* 3 times [42]
- 08. sc 3, inc, *sc 6, inc* 3 times, DG: sc 6, inc, sc 5, LG: sc, inc, sc 3 [48]
- 09. sc 7, inc, sc 2, W: sc 3, LG: sc 2, inc, *sc 7, inc* 4 times [54]
- 10. sc 4, inc, sc 5, W: sc 3, inc, sc, LG: sc 7, inc, *sc 8, inc* 3 times, sc 4 [60]

Attaching the Tail: Attach the tail where instructed while crocheting the next round.
- 11. sc 11, W: sc 7, LG: sc 2, DG: sc 22, Attach the tail in the next 5 stitches: (sc 5), sc 13 [60]

At the end of round 11, the tail should be centered above the legs on the opposite side of the round. If your tail appears off center, redo the round and adjust the placement of the tail as necessary.

- *12. sc 8, LG: sc 2, W: sc 9, LG: 41 [60]*
- *13. sc 10, W: sc 10, LG: sc 40 [60]*
- *14. sc 10, W: sc 11, LG: sc 2, DG: sc 37 [60]*
- *15. sc 8, LG: sc 2, W: sc 11, LG: sc 39 [60]*
- *16. sc 10, W: sc 11, LG: sc 39 [60]*
- *17. sc 10, W: sc 12, LG: sc 2, DG: sc 36 [60]*
- *18. sc 4, dec, sc 2, LG: sc 2, W: sc 4, dec, sc 6, LG: sc 2, dec, *sc 8, dec* 3 times, sc 4 [54]*
- *19. sc 9, W: sc 11, LG: 34 [54]*
- *20. sc 7, dec, sc, W: sc 6, dec, sc 2, LG: sc 2, DG: sc 3, dec, *sc 7, dec* 3 times [48]*
- *21. sc 7, LG: sc 2, W: sc 9, LG: sc 30 [48]*

- 22. sc 3, dec, sc 4, W: sc 2, dec, sc 5, LG: sc, dec, *sc 6, dec* 3 times, sc 3 [42]
- 23. sc 9, W: sc 7, LG: sc 2, DG: sc 24 [42]
- 24. sc 7, LG: sc 2, W: sc 7, LG: 26 [42]
- 25. sc 5, dec, sc 3, W: sc 2, dec, sc 2, LG: sc 3, dec, *sc 5, dec* 3 times [36]
- 26. sc 10, W: sc 4, LG: sc 2, DG: sc 20 [36]
- 27. sc 8, LG: sc 28 [36]
- 28. sc 2, dec, *sc 4, *dec* 5 times, sc 2 [30]
- 29. sc 22, DG: sc 8 [30]

Attaching the Arms: Attach the arms where instructed while crocheting the next round. .

- 30. LG: sc, Attach the first arm in the next six stitches: (sc 6), sc 8, Attach second arm in the next six stitches: (sc 6), sc 9 [30]

At the end of round 30, the arms should be centered above the legs and tail. If your arms appear off center, redo the round and adjust the placement of the arms as necessary. Stuff the body.

- 31. *sc 3, dec* 6 times [24]

Fasten off and leave a tail the length of your arm span (5+ feet).

TEDDY BEAR

This classic crochet teddy bear pattern is about 9 inches tall sitting and the perfect size for pretty much any age if you are looking to gift this sweet little teddy bear. This is a great pattern for advanced beginners, but even a determined beginner can make this work. This teddy bear is made to sit as a decoration or become a beloved crochet teddy bear toy.

Crochet Teddy Bear Materials
You will need:
- Approx 120 g size 4 yarn in main color
- Small amount of Ivory worsted weight
- Embroidery thread for eyebrows
- Crochet Hook in Size 3.75
- Tapestry Needle
- Polyfil
- 12mm safety eyes
- stitch marker

Crochet Teddy Bear Pattern Stitch Abbreviations
- SC– single crochet
- SC INC- single crochet increase (2 SC in each stitch)
- INV DEC– Invisible decrease (put hook through the FRONT LOOP ONLY of two consecutive stitches [two loops on hook] Yarn over pull through both loops. [two loops on hook] Yarn over pull through two loops)

33

- Magic Circle– Make a loop, leaving a long tail to work with. Insert hook in center of loop, yarn over and draw up a loop. Yarn over, pull through to make the first chain (this does not count as a stitch!). Continue to crochet over the loop and tail with the number of stitches called for. (If you need 6 SC, then crochet 6 SC inside the ring.) Pull the tail to close the circle.

INSTRUCTIONS

* Nose/Mouth
- Round 1: In a magic circle, 6 SC.
- Round 2: SC INC in each around. (12)
- Round 3: SC in first, SC INC in next. Repeat around. (18)
- Round 4: SC in first 2, SC INC in next. Repeat around. (24)
- Round 5: SC in first 3, SC INC in next. Repeat around. (30)
- Rounds 6-7: SC in each around. (30)
- Slip stitch in the next 3 stitches. Fasten off and leave a long tail to sew on to the face. Get a long piece of brown yarn. Sew the nose on about row 6. I make multiple passes (think 10-12) for this bear's nose. Try to use the same two holes when you go in and out. Use pins to attach it. For this bear, the snout will be more flat than full. Sew it around and very lightly stuff it.

* Body and Head
- Round 1: In a magic circle, 6 SC.
- Round 2: SC INC in each around. (12)
- Round 3: SC in first, SC INC in next. Repeat around. (18)
- Round 4: SC in first 2, SC INC in next. Repeat around. (24)

34

- Round 5: SC in first 3, SC INC in next. Repeat around. (30)
- Round 6: SC in first 4, SC INC in next. Repeat around. (36)
- Round 7: SC in first 5, SC INC in next. Repeat around. (42)
- Rounds 8-17: SC in each around. (42)
- Round 18: SC in first 5, INV DEC in the next. Repeat around. (36)
- Rounds 19-20: SC in each around. (36)
- Round 21: SC in first 4, INV DEC in the next. Repeat around. (30)
- Rounds 22-23: SC in each around. (30)

Begin stuffing here. Make sure you do not under-stuff.
- Round 24: SC in first 3, INV DEC in the next. Repeat around. (24)
- Rounds 25-26: SC in each around. (24)
- Round 27: SC in first 2, INV DEC in the next. Repeat around. (18)
- Round 28: SC in the first, INV DEC in the next. Repeat around. (12)

From here we are increasing the head.
- Round 29: SC in first, SC INC in next. Repeat around. (18)
- Round 30: SC in first 2, SC INC in next. Repeat around. (24)
- Round 31: SC in first 3, SC INC in next. Repeat around. (30)
- Round 32: SC in first 4, SC INC in next. Repeat around. (36)
- Round 33: SC in first 5, SC INC in next. Repeat around. (42)
- Round 34: SC in first 6, SC INC in next. Repeat around. (48)
- Rounds 35-45: SC in each around. (48)

Attach eyes between rows 39 and 41, about 6 stitches apart. Begin to stuff here. I also stretch the base of the head a little bit so it is more defined, more round than oval. Sew on the nose at this time as well.

- Round 46: SC in the first 6, INV DEC in the next. Repeat around. (42)
- Round 47: SC in the first 5, INV DEC in the next. Repeat around. (36)
- Round 48: SC in the first 4, INV DEC in the next. Repeat around. (30)
- Round 49: SC in the first 3, INV DEC in the next. Repeat around. (24)
- Round 50: SC in the first 2, INV DEC in the next. Repeat around. (18)
- Round 51: SC in the first, INV DEC in the next. Repeat around. (12)
- Round 52: INV DEC around. (6)

Fasten off and carefully sew the remaining hole closed.

* Arms

- *Round 1: 6 SC in a magic ring*
- *Round 2: SC INC in each around. (12)*
- *Round 3: SC in first, SC INC in next. Repeat around. (18)*
- *Round 4: SC in first 2, SC INC in next. Repeat around. (24)*
- *Rounds 5-8: SC in each around. (24)*
- *Round 9: SC in first 2, INV DEC in the next. Repeat around. (18)*
- *Round 10-22: SC in each around. (18)*
- *Round 23: SC in the first, INV DEC in the next. Repeat around.(12)*
- *Rounds 24: SC in each around. (12)*

Fasten off and leave a long tail. Pin the arms on each side the bear, about halfway just a couple of rounds beneath the head. Sew them on using the tail.

* Legs

- Round 1: 6 SC in a magic circle.
- Round 2: INC in each around. (12)
- Round 3: SC in the first, SC INC in the next. (18)
- Round 4: SC in the first 2, SC INC in the next. Repeat around. (24)
- Round 5: SC in first 3, SC INC in next. Repeat around. (30)
- Round 6: SC in first 4, SC INC in the next. Repeat around. (36)
- Rounds 7-11: SC in each around. (36)
- Round 12: INV DEC 12 times. SC in the remaining 12 stitches. (24)
- Round 13: INV DEC 6 times. SC in the remaining 12. (18)
- Rounds 14-25: SC in each around. (18)
- Round 26: SC in the first, INV DEC around. (12)
- Round 27: INV DEC in each around (6)

Fasten off and leave a long tail. Pin the legs on each side of the bottom of the bear, about halfway back. Sew them on using the tail.

* Ears (make 2)

- Round 1: 6 SC in a magic ring
- Round 2: SC INC in each around. (12)
- Round 3: SC in first, SC INC in next. Repeat around. (18)
- Round 4: SC in first 2, SC INC in next. Repeat around. (24)
- Round 5: SC in first 3, SC INC in next. Repeat around. (30)
- Rounds 6-7: SC in each around. (30)

Fasten off and leave a long tail. Flatten the ear. Attach about 5 rounds out from the middle of the head. Use pins to keep it in place. The ear will curve around so it looks more three dimensional. Attach it with the long tail.

DINOSAUR

You will need:

- Approx 120 g size 4 yarn in main color, approx 50g in accent
- Crochet Hook in Size 3.75
- Tapestry Needle
- Polyfil
- 10mm safety eyes
- stitch marker
- Embroidery thread for eye brows

Abbreviations (Written in US Terms)

- SC– single crochet
- SC INC– single crochet increase (2 SC in each stitch)
- INV DEC– Invisible decrease (put hook through the FRONT LOOP ONLY of two consecutive stitches [two loops on hook] Yarn over pull through both loops. [two loops on hook] Yarn over pull through two loops)
- Magic Circle– Make a loop, leaving a long tail to work with. Insert hook in center of loop, yarn over and draw up a loop. Yarn over, pull through to make the first chain (this does not count as a stitch!). Continue to crochet over the loop and tail with the number of stitches called for. (If you need 6 SC, then crochet 6 SC inside the ring.) Pull the tail to close the circle.

▪▪

INSTRUCTIONS

* Body

With main color:

- Round 1: In a magic circle, 6 SC.
- Round 2: SC INC in each around. (12)

- Round 3: SC in first, SC INC in next. Repeat around. (18)
- Round 4: SC in first 2, SC INC in next. Repeat around. (24)
- Round 5: SC in first 3, SC INC in next. Repeat around. (30)
- Round 6: SC in first 4, SC INC in next. Repeat around. (36)
- Round 7: SC in first 5, SC INC in next. Repeat around. (42)
- Round 8: SC in first 6, SC INC in next. Repeat around. (48)
- Round 9: SC in first 7, SC INC in next. Repeat around. (54)
- Rounds 10-18: SC in each around. (54)
- Round 19: SC in first 7, INV DEC in next. Repeat around. (48)
- Rounds 20: SC in each around. (48)
- Round 21: SC in the first 6, INV DEC in the next. Repeat around. (42)
- Round 22: SC in each around. (42)
- Round 23: SC in the first 5, INV DEC in the next. Repeat around. (36)
- Round 24: SC in each around. (36)
- Round 25: SC in the first 4, INV DEC in the next. Repeat around. (30)
- Round 26: SC in each around. (30)
- Round 27: SC in the first 3, INV DEC in the next. Repeat around. (24)
- Round 28: SC in each around. (24)
- Round 29 : SC in the first 2, INV DEC in the next. Repeat around. (18)
- Rounds 30-34: SC in each around (18)

Fasten off and leave a long tail to sew on the head.

* Head
(This will be the front of the nose. Begin with your choice of accent color.)

Chain 5. In the second chain from the hook SC. SC in the next 2. Place 3 SC in the last stitch on the row. On the other side of the chain, Sc in the next 2. Then 2 SC in the end stitch (the first stitch you SC on the chain). Place stitch marker (10)

HINT: It should look like this (every comma represents a stitch)

SC, SC, SC, 3 SC, SC, SC, 2 SC.

There will be 3 SC on the chain, with 3 SC on the end, 3 SC on the opposite side of the chain, and 3 SC total (first SC and then the 2 SC as you come back around) on the other end.

From here on we will be working in the round.

- Round 2: SC in first, SC INC in next. Repeat around. (15)
- Round 3: SC in first 2, SC INC in next. Repeat around. (20)
- Round 4: SC in first 3, SC INC in next. Repeat around. (25)
- Round 5: SC in first 4, SC INC in next. Repeat around. (30)
- Round 6: SC in first 5, SC INC in next. Repeat around. (35)
- Round 7: SC in first 6, SC INC in next. Repeat around. (40)
- Rounds 8-10: SC in each around. (40)

Switch to body color. For round 11, crochet in the back loops to make a neat color change on the nose. Resume a regular SC for Row 12 and on.

- Round 11: IN BACK LOOP ONLY SC in each around. (40)
- Rounds 12-20: SC in each around. (40)

Place eyes between rows 13 and 14. Sew on eyelashes or eyebrows here with the embroidery thread. Begin stuffing here.

- Round 21: SC in the first 6, INV DEC in the next. Repeat around. (35)
- Round 22: SC in the first 5, INV DEC in the next. Repeat around. (30)
- Round 23: SC in the first 4, INV DEC in the next. Repeat around. (25)
- Round 24: SC in the first 3, INV DEC in the next. Repeat around. (20)
- Round 25: SC in the first 2, INV DEC in the next. Repeat around. (15)
- Round 26: SC in the first 1, INV DEC in the next. Repeat around. (10)
- Round 27: INV DEC in each around. (5)

Using a needle sew up the remaining hole. Fasten off, weave in ends.

Legs (make 2)

- Round 1: In a magic circle, 6 SC.
- Round 2: SC INC in each around. (12)
- Round 3: SC in first, SC INC in next. Repeat around. (18)
- Round 4: SC in first 2, SC INC in next. Repeat around. (24)
- Round 5: SC in first 3, SC INC in next. Repeat around. (30)
- Rounds 6-10: SC in each around. (30)
- Round 11: SC in the first 3, INV DEC in the next. Repeat around. (24)
- Round 12: SC in the first 2, INV DEC in the next. Repeat around. (18)
- Round 13: SC in the first, INV DEC in the next. Repeat around. (12)

CHANGE COLOR

- Rounds 14-30: SC in each around (12)

Fasten off and leave a long tail to sew onto the body. Attach them in the middle, about 2 rows from the very center.

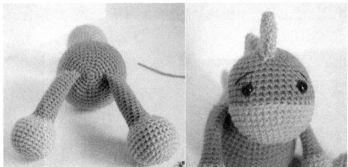

Arms (make 2)

- Round 1: In a magic circle, 6 SC.
- Round 2: SC INC in each around. (12)
- Round 3: SC in first, SC INC in next. Repeat around. (18)
- Rounds 4-6: SC in each around. (18)
- Round 7: SC in the first, INV DEC in the next. Repeat around. (12)

CHANGE COLOR

- Rounds 8-23: SC in each around (12)
- Fasten off and leave a long tail to sew onto the body. Attach them at an angle at around row 28 going down.

* Tail

- Round 1: 6 SC in a magic circle
- Round 2: SC in each around (6)
- Round 3: SC INC in each around (12)
- Round 4-6: SC in each around (12)
- Round 7: SC in the first, SC INC in the next. Repeat around. (18)
- Rounds 8-10: SC in each around. (18)

- Round 11: SC in first two, SC INC in the next. Repeat around. (24)
- Round 12-13: SC in each around. (24)
- Round 14: SC in first 3, SC INC in the next. Repeat around. (30)
- Rounds 15-22: SC in each around. (30)

Fasten off and leave a long tail to sew onto the body. Stuff the tail before sewing. To sew it on, sit the Dino on a flat surface. Lay the tail so that it is connected to the body and able to lay flat. Pin it in place and sew around.

* Spikes (make 5)
- Round 1: In a magic circle, 6 SC.
- Round 2: SC in each around. (6)
- Round 3: SC INC in each around. (12)
- Round 4: SC in first, SC INC in next. Repeat around. (18)
- Rounds 5-8: SC in each around. (18)

Fasten off and leave a long tail to sew on.

To attach, place all of the spikes on the Dino to ensure even spacing. I used pins.

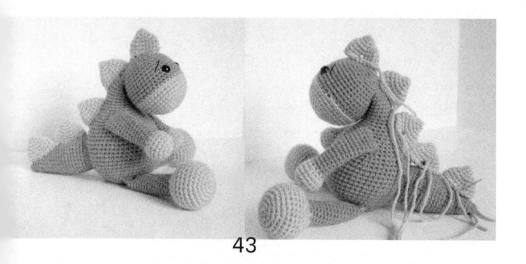

OCTOPUSES

This simple amigurumi octopus is quite quick to crochet. Make yours with a plain face, or add a little takochu mouth. They're stackable too, so you can make a whole tower of octopi.

Size:

Using medium (worsted) weight yarn and a 3.5 mm (E) crochet hook, your octopus will be about 4 cm / 1.6" wide. You can adjust the size by using thicker or thinner yarn.

Materials & tools:
• medium (worsted) weight yarn
• 3.5 mm (E) crochet hook
• small amount of stuffing
• 5 mm or 6 mm black beads for eyes (or safety eyes)
• black thread for sewing
• yarn needle and sewing needle

Abbreviations:
- ch = chain
- st = stitch
- sc = single crochet
- hdc = half double crochet
- sc2tog = single crochet 2 together
- sl st = slip stitch

* Body:

Start with a magic loop, or chain 2 and work in the first chain.

44

1. 6 sc in a circle.

2. 2 sc in each st around. (12 sc)

3. (sc in next st, 2 sc in next st) 6 times. (18 sc)

4. (sc in next st, 2 sc in next st, sc in next st) 6 times. (24 sc)

5-8. sc in each st around, for 4 rounds. (24 sc per round)

9. (sc2tog, sc in next st) 8 times. (16 sc)

Join round with a sl st.

10. Chain 1. Working in back loops only, (sc in next st, sc2tog, sc in next st) 4 times. (12 sc)

This creates a small ridge, that you'll use later when adding the legs.

11. Skip the ch1 that you made at the beginning of the previous round.

(sc2tog) 6 times. (6 sc)

Finish off, leaving a tail for sewing. Stuff the octopus body, and sew up the hole.

* Legs:

The octopus legs are made by crocheting into the row of 16 ridged stitches left on the body after round 10.

Holding the body with the top of the head facing downwards, join your yarn with a slip stitch. You can join in any one of the ridge stitches.

- 1. (5 hdc in next st, sl st in next st) 8 times. Join round with a sl st, and finish off.

You should have 8 little octopus legs now.

Takochu mouth (optional):

Start with a magic loop, or ch 2 and work in the first ch.

- 1. 6 sc in a circle. Join with a sl st, and finish off.

* Face:

For the plain face (purple octopus), sew the eyes onto your amigurumi's head. The eyes should be between the 7th and 8th rounds of the body, and about 5 stitches apart. Embroider a small black mouth.

For the takochu face (blue octopus), first sew the mouth in place. It should be roughly in line with the 6th and 7th rounds of the body. Sew the eyes on either side of the mouth, between the 6th and 7th rounds of the body.

DOLPHIN

Materials

- Himalaya baby dolphin yarn
- 4.5 mm crochet hook
- 10 mm safety eyes.

Abbreviations

- MR – Amigurumi Magic ring
- sc : Single Crochet
- hsc : Half single crochet
- inc : Increase
- dec : Decrease
- tr : Triple Crochet/ Treble Crochet

46

- st: Stitch
- dc : Double Crochet
- hdc: Half Double Crochet
- sl-st or Slst: Slip Stitch
- ch : Chain
- tch: Turnin chain crochet
- FLO : Crochet into front loops only
- BLO : Crochet into back loops only

BODY

Use Pink Yarn

- Row 1: 6sc in MR (6)
- Row 2: (1sc, 1inc) * 3 (9)
- Row 3: 9sc (9)
- Row 4: (2sc, 1inc) * 3 (12)
- Row 5: 3sc, 6inc, 3sc (18)
- Row 6: (2sc, 1inc) * 6 (24)
- Row 7: (3sc, 1inc) * 6 (30)
- Row 8 – Row 13: 30sc (30)
- Row 14: (3sc, 1dec) * 6 (24)
- Row 15: 24sc (24)
- Row 16: (2sc, 1dec) * 6 (18)
- Row 17: 6sc, (1sc, 1dec) * 4 (14)
- Row 18: 14sc (14)
- Row 19: (5sc, 1dec) * 2 (12)
- Row 20: 12sc (12)

Place the safety eyes between row 6 and 7 at about 8 sts (or 10 sts) apart.
Start stuffing with fiber fills firmly. Keep stuffing as you go.

- Row 21: (2sc, 1dec) * 3 (9)
- Row 22: 9sc (9)
- Row 23 (1sc, 1dec) * 3 (6)
- Row 24: 6sc (6)
- Row 25: 6inc (12)
- Row 26: 12inc (24)
- Row 27: 6sc, sk 12sts, 6sc (12)
- Row 28: (2sc, 1 dec) * 3 (9)
- Row 2g: (1sc, 1 dec) * 3 (6)
- Row 3o: 3dec (3)

Cut and secure the yarn.

Go back to row 27, use pink yarn, insert isc:

- Row 1: 12sc (12)
- Row 2: (2sc, 1dec) * 3 (g)
- Row 3: (isc, 1dec) * 3 (6)
- Row 4: 3dec (3)

Cut and secure the yarn.

FIN (Make 2) Use pink yarn

- Row 1: 4sc in MR (4)
- Row 2: 4sc (4)
- Row 3: 1sc, 2inc, 1sc (6)
- Row 4: 1sc, 4inc, 1sc (10)
- Row 5: 10sc (10)

Cut and secure the yarn. Sew the fin to the body

DORSAL FIN Use pink yarn

- Row 1: 4sc in MR (4)
- Row 2: 4sc (4)
- Row 3: 1sc, 2inc, 1sc (6)
- Row 4: 2sc, 2inc, 1sc, 1inc, 1sc (8)
- Row 5: 8sc (8)

Cut and secure the yarn. Sew the fin to the body.

BIRD

Abbreviations:

- BLO = Back Loop Only
- CH = Chain
- FLO = Front Loop Only
- FO = Finish Off
- MC = Magic Circle
- SC = Single Crochet
- SCDEC = Single Crochet Decrease
- SCINC = Single Crochet Increase
- SLST = Slip Stitch
- ST(S) = Stitches
- YO = Yarn Over

Supplies:

- 3.5 mm (E) Crochet Hook (or size needed to obtain gauge)
- Brava Worsted Weight Yarn (100% Premium Acrylic, Worsted Weight (4), 218yds/200m, 100g/3.5oz), 1 skein each of:
- Colour A: Tranquil (approx. 38 yds)
- Colour B: Mint (approx. 27 yds)
- Colour C: Canary (approx. 7 yds)
- 2 – 8 mm Safety Eyes
- Polyester Stuffing
- Scissors
- Tapestry Needle
- Stitch Marker

Special Stitches & Techniques:

Invisible Finish/Join: FO leaving a long tail. Thread the tail onto a tapestry needle. Place the tapestry needle through the top of the 2nd ST from front to back and pull through. Place tip of needle into top of the last ST of the round, under the back loop of the stitch, and pull through to the back of the work. Weave in the end.

NOTES:

Instructions within the brackets () are to be repeated the number of times specified next to the brackets.

This pattern is worked in continuous rounds (unless stated otherwise). Do not join at the end of the Round, unless indicated. A stitch marker is used to keep track of the beginning of the round.

For a cleaner SCDEC, do your SCDEC under the front loops only of each stitch rather than under both loops. This is often referred to as an invisible decrease.

Gauge is not vital to the project but it may affect the amount of yarn needed for the project and the size of your toy.

INSTRUCTIONS

* Body

- Round 1: Using Colour A, make a MC and SC 6 into the MC. (6)
- Round 2: (SCINC) x 6. (12)
- Round 3: (SC, SCINC) x 6. (18)
- Round 4: SC, SCINC, (SC 2, SCINC) x 5, SC. (24)
- Rounds 5 – 7: SC around. (24) – place safety eyes in Round 5 in STs 10 & 15.
- Round 8: (SC 3, SCINC) x 6. (30)

FO using invisible join (see special techniques). Join Colour B to the BLO of the first ST of Round 8.

- Round 9: SC in the BLO of the first ST and each ST around. (30)
- Round 10: SC 11, SCINC, (SC 2, SCINC) x 3, SC 9. (34)
- Rounds 11 – 15: SC around. (34)

- Round 16: SC 12, SCDEC, (SC 2, SCDEC) x 3, SC 8. (30)– Start stuffing, adding a bit more stuffing as you work. Stuff firmly.
- Round 17: (SC 3, SCDEC) x 6. (24)
- Round 18: SC, SCDEC, (SC 2, SCDEC) x 5, SC. (18)
- Round 19: (SC, SCDEC) x 6. (12)
- Round 20: (SCDEC) x 6. (6)

FO leaving a long tail. Finish stuffing. Thread tail onto tapestry needle and weave tail through FLO of last round and pull tight to close the hole. Weave in ends.

* Wings (Make 2)
- Round 1: Using Colour A, make a MC and SC 6 into the MC. (6)
- Round 2: (SCINC) x 6. (12)
- Round 3: (SC, SCINC) x 6. (18)
- Round 4: SC around. (18)
- Round 5: (SCDEC, SC 7) x 2. (16)
- Round 6: (SCDEC, SC 6) x 2. (14)
- Round 7: (SCDEC, SC 5) x 2. (12)
- Round 8: (SCDEC, SC 4) x 2. (10)
- Round 9: (SCDEC, SC 3) x 2. (8)
- Round 10: (SCDEC, SC 2) x 2. (6)

FO leaving a long tail. Flatten piece. Do NOT stuff. Thread tail onto tapestry needle and weave tail through FLO of last round and pull tight to close the hole.

Insert needle through center of last round and pull out through the side of the piece. Place a wing on either side of the body, with the tips of the wings pointing towards the back of the bird. When sewing the wings to the body, I recommend leaving the tips unsewn so they will stick out from the body. Sew the wings to the body.

* Beak

- Round 1: Using Colour C, make a MC and SC 3 into the MC. (3)
- Round 2: (SCINC) x 3. (6)
- Round 3: SC around. (6)

FO leaving a long tail. Flatten piece. Do NOT stuff. Sew beak onto the face, using photo as reference.

* Feet

- Row 1: Using 3.5mm hook and Brava Worsted, CH 3. In 2nd CH from hook, SC. SC in next ST. Turn. (2)
- Row 2: CH 1. SC in each ST. Turn. (2)
- Row 3: CH 1. SCINC in each ST. Turn. (4)
- Row 4: CH 4. SL ST in the 2nd CH from the hook. SL ST 2. SL ST in the next SC of Row 3. CH 4. SL ST in the 2nd CH from the hook. SL ST 2. SL ST in the next SC of Row 3. CH 4, SL ST in the 2nd CH from the hook. SL ST 2. SL ST in the last SC of Row 3. SL ST down the side of the foot, placing a SL ST in the end of each row.

FO leaving a long tail to sew onto body. Sew feet onto the bottom of the body so the toes just peek out the front.

* Tail

- Using Colour A, CH 8.
- Round 1: SCINC in the 2nd CH from the hook, SC in the next 5 STs, SC 5 in the last CH, working on the other side of the CH SC in the next 5 STs, SC 3 in the last ST. (20)
- Round 2: SC around. (20)
- Round 3: SCDEC, SC in the next 5 STs, SCDEC, SC in the next SC, SCDEC, SC in the next 5 STs, SCDEC, SC in the last. (16)
- Round 4: SC around. (16)

- Round 5: SCDEC, SC in the next 4 STs, (SCDEC) x 2, SC in the next 4 STs, SCDEC. (12)
- Round 6: SC around. (12)

FO leaving a long tail. Flatten piece. Do NOT stuff. Sew tail onto the bum. Weave in ends.

BUNNY RABBIT

The Crochet Bunny Rabbit is a crochet pattern that makes the perfect crochet baby shower gift, Easter basket stuffer, or nursery décor.

Crochet Stitches:
- Chain
- Magic Circle
- SC - Single Crochet
- INC - Single Crochet Increase
- DEC - Single Crochet Decrease
- Slip Stitch
- * - repeat sequence until the end of the round

* Bunny Legs and Torso:
- Round 1: In a magic circle, SC 6, pull tight (6 stitches)
- Round 2: INC in each stitch (12 stitches)
- Round 3: INC, SC in the next stitch* (18 stitches)
- Rounds 4-9: SC in each (18 stitches)`
- Chain 1, tie off with a medium tail and set aside.

Second Leg:
- Repeat Rounds 1-9 without tying off after Round 9
- Round 10: After the last stitch of round 9, SC directly into the 9th row of the other leg and continue to SC all the way around both legs (36 stitches)

53

- Rounds 11-13: SC in each stitch (36 stitches)

At this point, use a tapestry needle and the medium tail from the first leg and stitch together any opening between where we joined the legs. Tie off on the inside.

- Round 14: DEC, SC in the next 4* (30 stitches)
- Round 15: SC in each stitch (30 stitches)
- Round 16: DEC, SC in the next 4* (25 stitches)
- Rounds 17-19: SC in each stitch (25 stitches)
- Round 20: DEC, SC in the next 3* (20 stitches)
- Round 21: SC in each stitch (20 stitches)
- Round 22: DEC, SC in the next 3* (16 stitches)
- Round 23: DEC, SC in the next 2* (12 stitches)

Slip stitch, chain 1, tie off with a medium/short tail.
Add stuffing and set aside.

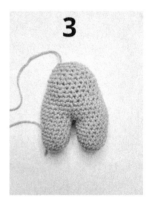

* Bunny Arms:

- Round 1: In a magic circle, SC 6, pull tight (6 stitches)
- Round 2: INC in each stitch (12 stitches)
- Rounds 3-14: SC in each stitch (12 stitches)
- Slip stitch, chain 1, tie off with a long tail.

Add very light stuffing, focusing on the bottom.
Using a tapestry needle and the long tails, attach the arms to the sides of the body.

* Bunny Head:
- Round 1: In a magic circle, SC 6, pull tight (6 stitches)
- Round 2: INC in each stitch (12 stitches)
- Round 3: INC, SC in the next stitch* (18 stitches)
- Round 4: INC, SC in the next 2 stitches* (24 stitches)
- Round 5: INC, SC in the next 3 stitches* (30 stitches)
- Round 6: INC, SC in the next 4 stitches* (36 stitches)
- Rounds 7-12: SC in each stitch (36 stitches)
- Round 13: DEC, SC in the next 4 stitches* (30 stitches)
- Round 14: DEC, SC in the next 3 stitches* (24 stitches)
- Round 15: DEC, SC in the next 2 stitches* (18 stitches)

Let's pause to add our safety eyes. I placed mine between the 11th and 12th rows, with 8 stitches in between.

- Using a tapestry needle and the yarn color of your choice, stitch on a cute little nose. I made a triangle shape between the eyes.
- And add some stuffing.
- Round 16: DEC, SC in the next stitch* (12 stitches)
- Round 17: DEC 6 times (6 stitches)
- Chain 1, tie off with a long tail.
- Using a tapestry needle and the long tail, stitch the remaining opening closed and attach to the body.

* Bunny Ears:
- Round 1: In a magic circle, SC 6, pull tight (6 stitches)
- Round 2: SC in each stitch (6 stitches)
- Round 3: INC, SC in the next stitch* (9 stitches)
- Rounds 4-5: SC in each stitch (9 stitches)
- Round 6: INC, SC in the next 2 stitches* (12 stitches)
- Rounds 7-16: SC in each stitch (12 stitches)

- Slip stitch, chain 1, tie off with a long tail.
- We won't be adding any stuffing to the ears so they'll sit relatively flat.

- To shape the ear, fold the bottom inward (sort of like a taco). Using a tapestry needle and the long tail, stitch the fold together.
- Again using the long tail and a tapestry needle, attach the ears to the head.

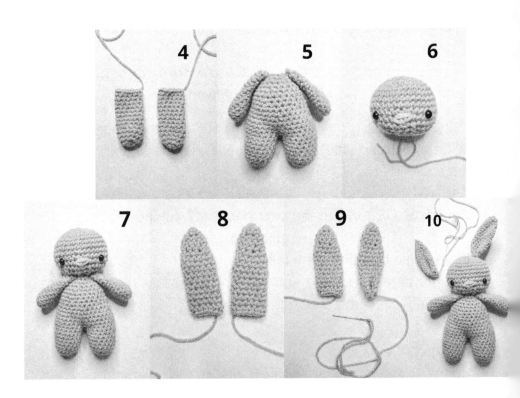

ELEPHANT

* Materials:

- DK weight yarn: approx. 100 grams in light gray, and 25 grams in dark gray
- 3.5mm crochet hook
- You can also try using worsted weight yarn & a 4 or 4.5mm hook, but the plushie size will vary depending on your tension.
- 12-mm black safety eyes (or embroider eyes for children under 3)
- Fiber Filling
- Yarn needle & stitch marker

* Gauge and Tension:

Exact gauge is not critical for this pattern. Keep tension normal—do not work with a loose tension. You can always adjust your hook size if need be. For example, if you crochet loosely and you find the amigurumi is looking holey, go down a hook size.

* Abbreviations/Stitches Used (U.S.)

- Chain – ch
- Slip stitch – sl st
- Single crochet – sc
- Half double crochet – hdc
- Repeat – rep
- Stitch(es) – st(s)
- Back loop single crochet – blsc
- Single crochet increase – inc
- Invisible decrease – inv dec
- Round – rnd

57

* Special Stitches:

- Invisible single crochet decrease (inv dec)
- Insert hook into front loop of first stitch, insert hook into front loop of the next stitch, yarn over, pull through both sts (2 loops on hook), yarn over and pull through all loops on hook to complete stitch.
- Single Crochet Increase (inc):
- Make 2 sc in indicated stitch.
- Half Double Crochet Increase (hdc inc):
- Make 2 hdc in indicated stitch.

* Legs – Make 2 in light gray

- Chart for first 3 rounds:

- Make a magic ring.
- Rnd 1: 8 sc into magic ring. (8)
- Rnd 2: Inc in each st around. (16)
- Rnd 3: (Inc, sc 1) x8. (24)
- Rnd 4: Blsc in each st around. (24)
- Rnd 5: Sc in each st around. (24)
- Rnd 6: (Sc 6, inv dec) x3. (21)
- Rnd 7: (Sc 5, inv dec) x3. (18)
- Rnd 8: (Sc 4, inv dec) x3. (15)
- Rnds 9-15: Sc in each st around. (15)

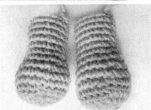

* Arms – Make 2 in light gray

- Make a magic ring.
- Rnd 1: 8 sc into the magic ring. (8)
- Rnd 2: Inc in each st around. (16)
- Rnd 3: (Inc in next st, sc 1) x8. (24)
- Rnd 4: Blsc in each st around. (24)
- Rnd 5: (Sc 4, inv dec) x3. Sc in last 6 sts. (21)
- Rnd 6: (Sc 3, inv dec) x3. Sc in last 6 sts. (18)
- Rnd 7: (Sc 2, inv dec) x3. Sc in last 6 sts. (15)

- First 7 rnds of arms:
- Rnds 8-12: Sc in each st around. (15)
- Rnd 13: (Sc 3, inv dec) x3. (12)
- Rnd 14: Sc in each st around. (12)
- Rnd 15: (Sc 2, inv dec) x3. (9)
- Rnds 16-17: Sc in each st around. (9)

Fasten off. Fill with stuffing until row 12. Sew the opening closed (see picture). Give the feet 3 "toes" by drawing a strand of yarn from below the blsc up to rnd 6. Do this twice, spaced apart by about 6 sts.

* Body – in light gray

- Make a magic ring.
- Rnd 1: 8 sc into magic ring. (8)
- Rnd 2: Inc in each st around. (16)
- Rnd 3: (Inc in next st, sc 1) x8. (24)
- Rnd 4: (Inc in next st, sc 2) x8. (32)
- Rnd 5: (Inc in next st, sc 3) x8. (40)
- Rnd 6: (Inc in next st, sc 4) x8. (48)
- Rnds 7-11: Sc in each st around. (48)
- Rnd 12: (Inv dec, sc 4) x8. (40)
- Rnds 13-14: Sc in each st around. (40)
- Rnd 15: (Inv dec, sc 3) x8. (32)
- Rnds 16-17: Sc in each st around. (32)
- Rnd 18: (Inv dec, sc 2) x8. (24)
- Rnd 19 and 20: Sc in each st around. (24)
- Fasten off. Fill with stuffing. Do not close the opening.

* Tail – in light gray and dark gray

- With light gray, ch 3.
- Rnd 1: 2 sc into the second ch from hook. 3 sc into next ch. Turn to work on the other side of the ch. 1 sc into other side of ch. (6)
- Rnds 2-10: Sc in each st around. (6)

59

Fasten off. Sew the opening closed (do not fill with stuffing). Cut some pieces of yarn from the dark gray and attach them into the first rnd of the tail like fringe.

* Trunk – in light gray

- Make a magic ring.
- Rnd 1: 8 sc into magic ring. (8)
- Rnd 2: Sc in each st around. (8)
- Rnd 3: Sl st in next 4 sts, sc 4. (8)
- Rnd 4: Sc in each st around. (8)
- Rnd 5: Rep round 3. (8)
- Rnd 6: Sl st in next 4 sts. Inc in each of the next 4 sts. (12)
- Rnd 7: Sl st in next 4 sts, sc 8. (12)
- Rnd 8: Sl st in next 4 sts, hdc 8. (12)
- Rnd 9: Sl st in next 4 sts. (Hdc 3, hdc inc) x2. (14)
- Rnd 10: Sc 4, hdc 10. (14)
- Rnd 11: Sl st in next 4 sts. (Hdc 4, hdc inc) x2. (16)
- Rnd 12: Sc 4, hdc 12. (16)
- Rnd 13: Sl st in next 4 sts. (Hdc 3, hdc inc) x3. (19)
- Rnd 14: Sc 4, hdc 15. (19)
- Rnd 15: Sl st in next 4 sts, hdc 15. (19)
- Rnd 16: Hdc in each st around. (19)

Fasten off. Fill with stuffing. Do not sew opening closed.

* Ears – Make 2 in dark gray & 2 in light gray

- Starting with dark gray yarn, make a magic ring.
- Row 1: Ch 2, 8 hdc into magic ring. Ch 2 and turn. (8)
- Row 2: Make 2 hdc in each st. Ch 2 and turn. (16)
- Row 3: (Hdc 1, 2 hdc in next st) x8. Ch 2 and turn. (24)
- Row 4: (Hdc 2, 2 hdc in next st) x8. (32)

For light gray ears, follow rnds 1 to 4 above. Do not fasten off. Place the dark gray ear on top of the light gray ear and work into both pieces together. Work the following rnd below to join them together.

Joining Row: Ch 1, sc in next 7 sts (working through the layers of both ears). 4 sc in next st. Sc in next 16 sts, 4 sc in next st. Sc in last 7 sts. Fasten off.
Placing the dark gray ear on the light gray ear and working into both pieces together:

* Head – in light gray

- Make a magic ring.
- Rnd 1: 8 sc into magic ring. (8)
- Rnd 2: Inc in each st around. (16)
- Rnd 3: (Inc in next st, sc 1) x8. (24)
- Rnd 4: (Inc in next st, sc 2) x8. (32)
- Rnd 5: (Inc in next st, sc 3) x8. (40)
- Rnd 6: (Inc in next st, sc 4) x8. (48)
- Rnds 7-12: Sc in each st around. (48)

Attach eyes between round 4 and 5, with 10 sts in between them.
- Rnd 13: (Sc 6, inv dec) x6. (42)
- Rnd 14: (Sc 5, inv dec) x6. (36)

- Rnd 15: (Sc 4, inv dec) x6. (30)
- Rnd 16: (Sc 3, inv dec) x6. (24)
- Rnd 17: (Sc 2, inv dec) x6. (18)
- Begin stuffing here.
- Rnd 18: (Sc 1, inv dec) x6. (12)
- Rnd 19: (Inv dec over next 2 sts) x6. (6)

Fasten off. Fill with stuffing. Sew the opening closed.

Finishing:

Attach trunk and ears to the head.

Join head and body together.

Attach arms, legs, and tail.

BEES

- US G6/4mm crochet hook.
- 1/4 oz each of Yellow, Black and Ivory color yarn, I used Hobby Lobby I Love This Cotton in Black, Curry and Ivory
- 6mm safety eyes
- tapestry needle and scissors.
- Size: 2-1/2" long (end to end) by 2" tall (from bottom of belly to tip of wing)

* Body

- With yellow yarn, make a magic ring

- R1: 6 sc into ring (6 sts).
- R2: 2 sc in ea st around (12 st)
- R3: *sc in next st, 2 sc in next st, repeat from * around (18 st)
- R4-5: sc around (18 st) Change to black in very last stitch.
- R6-7: With black, sc around. Change to yellow in last stitch

- R8-11: With yellow, sc around (18 st) Change to black in last stitch
- R12: With black, sc around. (18 st)

Take time out to insert safety eyes. The safety eyes go between rounds 2 & 3 and there are about 7 stitches in between. Refer to photo for placement. Stuff bee body with toy stuffing and continue stuffing as you finish up the body.

- R13: *sc in next st, sc next 2 st together. Repeat from * around (12)
- R14: sc next 2 st together (6).
- R15: sc next 2 st together (3). Fasten off, leaving a long strand for sewing. Make sure bee is firmly stuffed, then thread the yarn end onto the tapestry needle. Weave opening closed. Fasten off and weave in end.

* Wings (make 2)

- The wings are made by making a magic ring and working several stitches into the magic ring as follows:
- With ivory color yarn, make a magic ring.

- R1: Inside the ring, work the following: sc, hdc, dc, 3 tr, dc, hdc, sc. Cut yarn, leaving some length for sewing, using an invisible join, attach the end and start of the wing together. Weave in end to make join secure, then sew the wing onto the top of the body. Repeat for the 2nd wing.

RATTLE FROG

Necessary materials :
– YarnArt Jeans (55% cotton, 45% acrylic, 50gr/160m): green (#69), white (#62), red (56)

Hook #2
– Eyelets on a 9mm safety mount
– Rattler
– Filler (holofiber or sintepukh)
– Wooden ring
– Black sewing thread for mouth decoration
– Needle for sewing details
– Scissors

- Abbreviations
- AR - Amigurumi Magic ring
- MR-Amigurumi Magic ring
- 3in1 - crochet 3 columns in one loop
- sc: Single Crochet
- inc: Increase
- dec: Decrease
- tr: Triple Crochet/ Treble Crochet
- st: Stitch
- dc: Double Crochet
- hdc: Half Double Crochet
- sl-st or Slst: Slip Stitch
- ch: Chain

- tch: Turnin chain crochet
- ..in : make increase into same stitch as many as the number which is given in front of "inc"
- abbreviation (exp; 3inc, 4inc..).
- FLO: Crochet into front loops only
- BLO: Crochet into back loops only

* Head

- 1. 6 sc in MR
- 2.6 inc (12)
- 3. (1sc,inc)*6 (18)
- 4. 1sc, inc, (2sc,inc)*5, 1sc (24)
- 5. (3sc,inc)*6 (30)

- 6. 2sc, inc, (4sc, inc)*5, 2sc (36)
- 7. (5sc,inc)*6 (42)
- 8. 3sc, inc, (6sc,inc)*5, 3sc (48)
- 9-18. 48ss (10 rows)
- 19. 3sc, dec, (6sc, dec)*5, 3sc(42)
- 20. (5sc,dec)*6 (36)
- at this stage it is convenient to start stuffing the part and insert the rattle

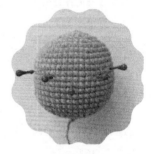

- 21. 2sc, dec, (4sc, dec)*5, 2sc (30)
- 22. (3sc, dec)*6 (24)
- 23. 1sc, dec, (2sc, dec)*5, 1sc (18)
- 24. (1sc,dec)*6 (12)
- 25. 6dec (6)
- Pull the hole with a needle, leave the thread for sewing to the base. We outline the points along which we will embroider the mouth:

- The central one (the very bottom of the mouth) is located between the 13th and 14th rows;
- From it, 1 row higher (between 12 and 13 rows) are the middle points between them, the distance is 6 columns;
- And the top ones 1 row higher (between 11 and 12 rows) are the corners of the mouth between them, the distance is 10 loops.
- Embroider the mouth with black thread.

65

* Eyes

- We crochet with white yarn
- 1. 6sc in MR
- 2. 6inc (12)
- 3. (1sc, inc)*6 (18), slst
- fasten and cut the thread In the center we insert the eyes on a safe mount,
- We crochet with green yarn
- 1. 6sc in MR
- 2. 6inc (12)
- 3. (1sc,inc)*6 (18)
- 4.-6. 18sc (3 rnds)

We attach a piece of white yarn to the part from green yarn and crochet 18sc

Sew on the eyes.
Wooden side.
We collect a chain of 25 ch, from the second loop from the hook we begin to crochet 24 sc, ch;We turn crocheting and crochet 24 sc, ch again

GAZELLA AHU

Insert your safety eyes 8 mm on round 10/11 with a distance of 18 holes.

• Eyes are symmetrical to the middle of the head.

 Sew a little nose on round 1/2

- This pattern is an intermediate pattern.

- I used for the optimal result alize alpaca (nearly 60 g)

- Hook size: 2.2 mm tulip

- For the embroidery I used catania.

- The size of Ahu is about 15 cm, if you use the suggested yarn.

* Head

- Rnd 1.6 sc in MR (6)
- Rnd 2.(1 sc, 1 inc)*3 (9)
- Rnd 3.(2 sc, 1 inc)*3 (12)
- Rnd 4.(3 sc, 1 inc)*3 (15)
- Rnd 5.(4 sc, 1 inc)*3 (18)
- Rnd 6.(5 sc, 1 inc)*3 (21)
- Rnd 7.(2 sc, 1 inc, 3 sc, 1 inc)*3 (27)
- Rnd 8.7 sc, (3 inc), 17 SC (30)
- Rnd 9.8 SC, 6 inc), 16 SC (36)

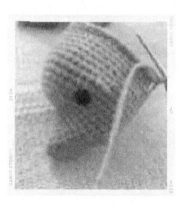

- Rnd 10.(4 sc, 1 inc)*2, 9 sc, 1 inc, 4 sc, 1 inc, 11 sc (40)
- Rnd 11.sc around (40)
- Rnd 12.(5 sc, 1 inc)*2, 10 sc, 1 inc, 5 sc, 1 inc, 11 sc (44)
- Rnd 13.sc around (44)

- Rnd 14.(6 sc, 1 inc)*2, 11 sc, 1 inc, 6 sc, 1 inc, 11 sc (48)
- Rnd 15.sc around (48)
- Rnd 16.(6 sc, 1 dec)*2, 11 sc, 1 dec, 6 sc, 1 dec, 11 sc (44)
- Rnd 17.sc around (44)
- Rnd 18.sc around (44)
- Rnd 19.13 sc, 1 dec, 11 sc, 1 dec, 16 SC (42)
- Rnd 20.sc around (42)
- Rnd 21.(5 sc, 1 dec)*6 (36)
- Rnd 22.(4 sc, 1 dec)*6 (30)
- Rnd 23.(3 sc, 1 dec)*6 (24)
- Rnd 24.(2 sc, 1 dec)*6 (18)
- Rnd 25.(1 sc, 1 dec)*6 (12)
- Rnd 26.(dec)*6 (6)

* Body

- (we start from the neck) -leave a long tail, for sewing later-
- Rnd 1.ch 18 (make a ring without twisting it)
- Rnd 2-5.sc around (18) *4 rounds
- Rnd 6.now we chain 18 ch (this will be the back)
- Rnd 7.crochet from the 2nd ch from your hook 17 sc on the chain, 18 sc on the neck and 17 sc from the other side of the chain (52)
- Rnd 8.mark the next stitch (this is your beginning) (inc) x 2, 21 sc, 1 inc, 4 sc, 1 inc, 22 sc, 1 inc (57)
- Rnd 9.(1 sc, 1 inc) x 2, 49 sc, (1 sc, 1 inc)*2 (61)
- Rnd 10.5 sc, 1 inc, 22 sc, 1 inc, 5 sc, 1 inc, 23 sc, 1 inc, 2 sc (65)
- Rnd 11.1 sc, 1 inc, 4 sc, 1 inc, 23 sc, 1 inc, 6 sc, 1 inc, 24 sc, 1 inc, 2 sc (70)
- Rnd 12-14.sc around (70) *3 rounds
- Rnd 15.1 sc, 1 dec, 5 sc, 1 dec, 23 sc, 1 dec, 6 sc, 1 dec, 20 sc, 1 dec, 5 SC (65)

- Rnd 16.sc around (65)
- Rnd 17.2 sc, 1 dec, 3 sc, 1 dec, 22 sc, 1 dec, 5 sc, 1 dec, 19 sc, 1 dec, 5 sc (60)
- Rnd 18-20.sc around (60) *3 rounds

* **Belly** (crochet with white yarn)

- count 5 sc from the last stitch you've made on your body and join in:
- Rnd 1.24 sc
- Rnd 2.ch 1, turn 24 sc
- Rnd 3-9.24 sc *7 rows

Sew the belly to the body. Spit 6 stitches of the body part - and join into the 7th.

Make sure to stuff your body firmly.

* **Ears**

- Rnd 1.4 sc in MR (4)
- Rnd 2.(1 sc, 1 inc)*2 (6)
- Rnd 3.(1 sc, 1 inc)*3 (9)
- Rnd 4.(2 sc, 1 inc)*3 (12)
- Rnd 5.(3 sc, 1 inc)*3 (15)
- Rnd 6.sc around (15)
- Rnd 7.(3 sc, 1 dec)*3 (12)

Embroider with white and black yarn

Sew them on round 17/18 symmetrical to the eyes

* Tail

- Rnd 1.4 sc in MR (4)
- Rnd 2.(1 sc, 1 inc)* 2 (6)
- Rnd 3.(1 sc, 1 inc)*3 (9)
- Rnd 4.(2 sc, 1 inc)*3 (12)
- Rnd 5.sc around (12)
- Rnd 6.1 ch, turn and crochet both sides together (6)• Sew the tail in the middle of the back on round 4/5.

* Legs (start with dark brown)

- Rnd 1. 6 sc in MR (6)
- Rnd 2. (inc)*6 (12)
- Rnd 3. in BLO SC around (12)
- Rnd 4. sc around (12)(change to light brown)
- Rnd 5. in BLO sc around (12)
- Rnd 6-11. sc around (12)*6 rounds
- Rnd 12. crochet both sides together with 1 ch, 6 SC (6)
- Rnd 13. now you have to turn and crochet on both sides only in FLO (12)
- Rnd 14-21. sc around (12) *8 rounds
- Rnd 22. (2 sc, 1 inc)*4 (16)
- Rnd 23. (3 sc, 1 inc)*4 (20)
- Rnd 24. sc around (20)
- Rnd 25. (dec)*10 (10)
- Rnd 26.(dec)*5 (5)

Stuff the legs lightly • Sew them with a movable stitch on round 14/15 (counting from the neck to the belly(brown)• You can sew buttons on the legs

DOG

* Materials

- Yarnart Jeans yarn.
- Eyes 6mm
- The size of the toy is 13cm.

* Abbreviations

- MR: Amigurumi Magic ring
- sc: Single Crochet
- inc: Increase
- dec: Decrease
- trc: Triple Crochet/ Treble Crochet
- st: Stitch
- dc: Double Crochet
- hdc: Half Double Crochet
- sist: Slip Stitch
- ch: Chain
- ..in : make increase into same stitch as many as the number which is given in front of
- "inc" abbreviation (exp; 3inc, 4inc..).
- FLO: Crochet into front loops only
- BLO: Crochet into back loops only

* Head

- 1) Black yarn – 6 sc Then everything is brown
- 2) 6 sc
- 3) (2 sc, inc) *2 (8 sc)
- 4) (3 sc, inc) *2 (10 sc)
- 5) (4 sc, inc) *2 (12 sc) we stuff the part in the crocheting process

6) 12 sc

7) (3 sc, inc) *3 (15 sc)

8) (4 sc, inc) *3 (18 sc)

9) (2 sc, inc) *6 (24 sc) sew eyes in rows 10-11

10) 9 sc, 6 inc, 9 sc (30 sc)

11) 9 sc, (1 sc, inc) *6, 9 sc (36 sc)

12-15) 36 sc

16) (4 sc, dec) *6 (30 sc) eyes - beads, 6mm.

17) 30 sc

18) (3 sc, dec) *6 (24 sc)

19) (2 sc, dec) *6 (18 sc)

20) (1 sc, dec) *6 (12 sc)

21) 6 dec. Pull off the hole, leave a long yarn for sewing.

* Ears

1) 6 sc

2) 6 inc (12 sc)

3) (1 sc, inc) * 6 (18 sc)

4) 18 sc

5) (4 sc, dec) *3 (1 5 sc)

6) 15 sc

7) (3 sc, inc) *3 (12 sc)

8) 12sc

9) (4 sc, dec) *2 (10 sc)

10-12) 10 sc

Fold in half, Crochet at both ends 5 sc.

* Hands (Brown yarn)

1) 6 in MR

2) 6 inc (12 sc)

3) 12 sc

4) (2 sc, dec) *3 (9 sc)

Change the yarn to the color of the jacket

5-8) 9 sc

9) dec, 7 sc (8 sc)

10-11) 8 sc

Fill part a little, fold in half, crochet on both sides 4 sc.

* Legs

1) Brown yarn6 sc in MR.

2) 6 inc (12 sc)

3) (1 sc, inc) *6 (18 sc)

4-5) 18 sc

6) (1 sc, dec) *6 (12 sc)

Change to pants color

72

7-10) 12 sc

Crochet one leg, cut the yarn, fasten. Crochet the second, continue without cutting the yarn - Collect 3 ch and attach to the first leg.

11) 12 sc on the leg, 3 sc in a chain of 3 ch, 12 sc on the leg, 3 sc in a chain of 3 ch.

12-15) 30 sc

Change the yarn to the color of the jacket. We do not cut the yarn from the pants, but bring it forward

16) (3 sc, dec) *6 (24 sc) Crochet the row BLO

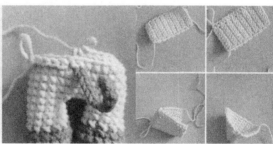

Return to pants and tie 30 sc at the front half loop. Cut the varn. fasten.

17-20) 24 sc

21) (2 sc, dec) *6 (18 sc)

22) 18 sc

23) Crochet hands in this row 3 sc, 4 sc with hand, 5 sc, 4 sc with hand, 2 sc (18 sc)

24) 18 sc

Cut the yarn, fasten. Fill in the detail.

* Hood

Leave a long yarn. It will be needed to sew on the hood. Cast on 10 sc, from secondloop from hook to 9 sc along the chain. Next, make 1 ch and rotate crochetting.crochet 9 sc and so on. There should be 1 b rows in total. After the last row has beentied, tie the long edge (see photo) then fold the edges with the short side and crochetconnecting posts at both edges. Sew the hood to the body. Sew on the head, ears.

CHICKEN

Materials:

Crochet a larger or smaller version of this small chicken amigurumi you can just use a thicker or thinner yarn/crochet hook.

Cotton Sport Weight version 6 cm/2 inch:

- Red catania cotton color - 115
- Yellow catania cotton color - 208
- White catania cotton color - 105
- Black catania cotton color - 110
- Synthetic Poly filling

Chenille Super Bulky version 12 cm / 5 inch:

- Red Chenille yarn
- Yellow Chenille yarn
- White Chenille yarn
- Black Chenille yarn
- Synthetic Poly filling

Supplies:

- Scissors
- Tapestry needles with blunt point, nr. 16 or 17
- Pins
- Crochet hook size 2.5 mm 4/0 for the cotton or 5.0 mm H for Chenille yarn

Body:

Use white yarn
- Rnd 1: start 6 sc in a magic ring (6)
- Rnd 2: inc 6 times (12)
- Rnd 3: (sc in next 3, inc in next st) repeat 3 times (15)

Mark the beginning of round 5 with a piece of yarn if you haven't already, so you can count the stitches later.

- Rnd 4-5: sc in all 15 st (15)

If you want you can turn the chicken into a keychain by sewing two strands of folded yarn in the top and secure it on the inside of the body (in the video I do this a bit later, but doing it now is easier.)

- Rnd 6: (sc in next 4, inc in next st) repeat 3 times (18)

74

- Rnd 7: ch 4, Start in second ch from hook, sc in next 21 stitches (21+31)
- Rnd 8: sc in next 3, inc, sc in next 5 st, inc, sc in next 2 st, inc, sc in next 1 st, inc, sc in next 1 st, inc, sc in next 2 st, inc, sc in next 4 st (30)
- Rnd 9-11: sc in all 30 st (30)
- Rnd 12: sc in next 1 st, dec 3 times, sc in next 4 st, dec, sc in next 2 st, dec, sc in next 1 st, dec, sc in next 1 st, dec, sc in next 2 st, dec, sc in next 1 st, dec (21)
- Rnd 13: dec, sc in next st, dec 2 times, sc in next 14 st (18)
- Sew the eyes on round 5, one eye between the 4th and 5th stitch and the other between the 9th and 10th stitch.

Stuff the body with toy fiberfilling and continue stuffing as you go.
- Rnd 14: (sc in next st, dec) repeat 6 times (12)
- Rnd 15: dec 6 times (6)

Finish the head by taking the last strand of yarn and sewing it through the front loops of every crochet stitch that you made in the last round. Pull the yarn tight to close the hole. Now stick a needle under the hole and weave in the yarn end.

Beak: in yellow yarn
- Rnd 1: start 6 sc in a magic ring (6)
- Fasten off, leaving a long tail for sewing.
- Sew the beak on rounds 5 and 6 of the body.

Comb part 1: in red yarn
- Rnd 1: start sc 7 in a magic circle (7)
- Rnd 2: sc in all 7 st (7)
- Fasten off, leaving a long tail for sewing.

Comb part 2 : in red yarn
- Rnd 1: start sc 5 in a magic circle (7)
- Rnd 2: sc in all 5 st (5)
- Fasten off, leaving a long tail for sewing.

- Both comb parts are sewed over round 1 and 2, comb part 1 is sewed on the front of the body, and comb part 2 on the back.

Wings 2x: in white yarn
- Rnd 1: start 6 sc in a magic ring (6)
- Rnd 2: inc 2 times, hdc + dc + hdc in next st, inc 3 times (13)
- Fasten off, leaving a long tail for sewing.
- Sew the wings on the side of the body. The wings are sewed below the sixth round.

Now your chicken is done!

LADYBUGS

MATERIALS
- 4mm crochet hook
- Stitch marker
- Tapestry needle
- 10mm safety eyes
- Poly-fil stuffing
- Red Heart Super Saver Yarn, Turqua (26 yds), Bright Yellow (1.5 yds), White (2 yds)
- Scissors
- Pins (optional)
- Rather not assemble the materials yourself? Buy a Penguin Crochet Kit instead

NOTES
- This pattern is written in US terminology, and crocheted in the round.
- While pins are optional, they are recommended since it makes it much easier to plan and sew on the amigurumi pieces,
- If you use worsted-weight yarn and a 4.0mm hook, the penguin will come out to 3.5 in (8.9 cm) tall. It'll nestle quite nicely in the palm of your hand!

TERMINOLOGY

- sc: single crochet
- inc: increase stitch (2 sc in 1 stitch of the previous round)
- dec: (invisible) decrease
- magic loop: also known as a magic ring
- rnd: round
- [sc, inc] x 3: 1 sc followed by 1 inc, repeated 3 times
- (6 sts): 6 total stitches in the round

HEAD & BODY

- Use blue yarn.
- Rnd 1: 6 sc in magic loop (6 sts)

- To keep track of where you are, use a stitch marker to mark the beginning of each rnd. Each time you start a new rnd, move the stitch marker to the first stitch of that rnd.

- Rnd 2: inc x 6 (12 sts)
- Rnd 3: [sc, inc] x 6 (18 sts)
- Rnd 4: [inc, 2 sc] x 6 (24 sts)
- Rnd 5: 24 sc (24 sts)

- Your work might start curling at this point. For a neater final look, flip it inside out so that the "right side" faces out.

- Rnd 6: [5 sc, inc] x 4 (28 sts)
- Rnd 7-9: 28 sc (28 sts)
- Rnd 10: [6 sc, inc] x 4 (32 sts)
- Rnd 11-13: 32 sc (32 sts)
- Rnd 14: [2 sc, dec] x 8 (24 sts)
- Rnd 15: 24 sc (24 sts)
- Rnd 16: [sc, dec] x 8 (16 sts)
- Rnd 17: 16 sc (16 sts)

Insert the safety eyes between rnds 7 & 8, with 6 stitches between them. Stuff your piece, shaping it like an egg.

77

- Rnd 18: dec x 8 (8 sts)

BELLY

- Use white yarn.
- Rnd 1: 6 sc in magic loop (6 sts)
- Rnd 2: inc x 6 (12 sts)
- Rnd 3: [sc, inc] x 6 (18 sts)
- Rnd 4: [inc, 2 sc] x 6 (24 sts)
- Fasten off. Attach the top of the belly to the body between rnds 9 & 10.

BEAK: Use yellow yarn.

- Rnd 1: 4 sc in magic loop (4 sts)
- Rnd 2: [sc, inc] x 2 (6 sts)
- Fasten off and don't stuff. Attach the beak between rnds 7 & 8, starting at the middle of the eyes and ending right above the belly.

WINGS: Use blue yarn. Make two.

- Rnd 1: 4 sc in magic loop (4 sts)
- Rnd 2: inc x 4 (8 sts)
- Rnd 3: 8 sc (8 sts)
- Fasten off and don't stuff. Sl st, ch 1. Flatten the wing with the ch stitch on the right side of the wing, and single crochet together the stitches that are across from each other:
- Attach the wings between rnds 9 & 10, where the beak and belly meet.

78

LADYBUGS

Materials

- Crochet hook size 2.50mm
- Darning needle for finishing
- Possibly stitch markers and row/round counter
- Stuffing/fibrefill

Yarn consumption

- Shamrock Yarns 100% Cotton 8/4
- Shamrock yarns 100% cotton – 8/4, colour 01 – black, 7 grams
- Shamrock yarns 100% cotton – 8/4, colour 03 – off white, 1 gram
- Shamrock yarns 100% cotton – 8/4, colour 21 – dark Christmas red, 9 grams

Abbreviations

- dc - double crochet
- ch - chain stitches
- sl st - slip stitch
- inc - increase (2 stitches in the same stitch)
- dec – decrease (crochet 2 stitches together)

Instructions

The body

- Start with colour 21 dark Christmas red
- Start by making 6 dc in a magic ring
- Inc x 6 (12)
- 1 dc, inc x 6 (18)
- 2 dc, inc x 6 (24)
- 3 dc, inc x 6 (30)
- 4 dc, inc x 6 (36)
- 5 dc, inc x 6 (42)

79

- Make 5 rounds of 42 dc, change to black on the last stitch.

For the next round, you only crochet in the back loop, and afterwards, you do both again.

- 5 dc, dec x 6 (36)
- 4 dc, dec x 6 (30)
- 3 dc, dec x 6 (24)
- 2 dc, dec x 6 (18)
- 1 dc, dec x 6 (12)
- Stuff the body with fibrefill

- Dec x 6 (6)
- Weave the last 6 stitches together and cut the yarn, leaving a long tail.
- You use this strand to divide the body in two by the wings of the ladybug.
- Bring the crochet hook through the middle of the magic ring, around the yarn and back down again. This way you are fastening the dividing strand to the body. Weave in the end.

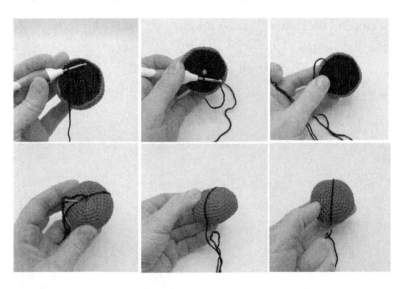

The Head

- Start by making 6 dc in a magic ring.
- Inc x 6 (12)
- 1 dc, inc x 6 (18)
- 2, dc, inc x 6 (24)
- Crochet 3 rounds of 24 dc

Crochet a slip stitch, cut the yarn, but leave a long tail for sewing the head onto the body.

Sew the head onto the body. Add filling to the head before you finish sewing.

Weave in the ends.

Dots: You make 7 dots.

- Make 6 dc in a magic ring
- Cut the yarn, leaving a long tail for sewing on the dots.
- You now embroider the eyes on your ladybug. Cut a long strand from the yarn in the off-white colour.
- Once you have embroidered the eyes, you weave in the ends.

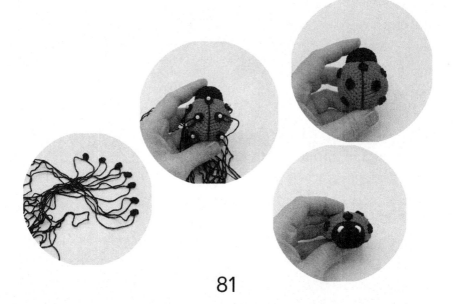

SQUIRRELS

Materials

- Red Heart Soft worsted weight yarn, 100% acrylic, 256 yds / 5 oz / 141 g, 1 ball (20 yds) #E728 Cocoa (MC), < 1 ball #7933 Wheat (AC1)
- Red Heart Hygge bulky yarn, 70% acrylic, 30% nylon, 132 yds / 5 oz / 141 g, 1 ball #E869 Latte (AC2).

- G (4.25 mm) crochet hook
- Two 15 mm brown safety eyes
- Fairfiled Poly-Fil Fiber Filling
- Tapestry needle
- Straight pins
- Stitch markers (if desired)

Gauge

- Gauge is not important for amigurumi. Be sure to use the same hook throughout to ensure proportional size.

Abbreviations Used in This Pattern

- ( )Repeat instructions between brackets as indicated.
- AC1 – Accent Color 1
- AC2 – Accent Color 2
- ch – chain
- dec – decrease (sc2tog)
- inc – increase (2 sc in next st)
- MC – Main Color
- sc – single crochet
- sc join – With slip knot on hook, insert hook into stitch, yo, pull up a loop, yo pull through both loops on hook.
- sl st – slip stitch

Pattern Notes

- Work in continuous rounds unless otherwise specified by pattern.

82

- For best results, assemble parts in order specified by pattern.
- Do not weave in ends of each part until the end. This allows for repositioning of parts if needed.
- Ch-3 at beginning of round counts as dc.

Body

- With MC, ch 2.
- Rnd 1: 6 sc in second ch from hook. (6)
- Rnd 2: Inc in each st around. (12)
- Rnd 3: [sc, inc] 6 times. (18)
- Rnd 4: [2 sc, inc] 6 times. (24)
- Rnd 5: 12 sc, change to AC1, 12 sc. (24)
- Rnd 6: Change to MC, [3 sc, inc] 3 times, change to AC1, [3 sc, inc] 3 times. (30)
- Rnd 7: Change to MC, 15 sc, change to AC1, 15 sc. (30)
- Rnd 8: Change to MC, [4 sc, inc] 3 times, change to AC1, [4 sc, inc] 3 times. (36)
- Rnd 9: Change to MC, 18 sc, change to AC1, 18 sc. (36)
- Rnd 10: Change to MC, [5 sc, inc] 3 times, change to AC1, [5 sc, inc] 3 times. (42)
- Rnd 11: Change to MC, 21 sc, change to AC1, 21 sc. (42)
- Rnd 12: Change to MC, [6 sc, inc] 3 times, change to AC1, [6 sc, inc] 3 times. (48)
- Rnds 13-20: Change to MC, 24 sc, change to AC1, 24 sc. (48)
- Rnd 21: Change to MC, [6 sc, dec] 3 times, change to AC1, [6 sc, dec] 3 times. (42)
- Rnd 22: Change to MC, [5 sc, dec] 3 times, change to AC1, [5 sc, dec] 3 times. (36)
- Rnd 23: Change to MC, [4 sc, dec] 3 times, change to AC1, [4 sc, dec] 3 times. (30)
- Rnd 24: Change to MC, [3 sc, dec] 6 times. (24)
- Rnd 25: [2 sc, dec] 6 times. (18)
- Stuff.

83

- Rnd 26: [sc, dec] 6 times. (12)
- Rnd 27: Dec 6 times. (6)

Bind off leaving long tail for sewing. Thread tail through remaining 6 sts, pull tight to close. Weave in ends.

Head

- With MC, ch 2.
- Rnd 1: 6 sc in second ch from hook. (6)
- Rnd 2: Inc in each st around. (12)
- Rnd 3: [2 sc, inc] 4 times. (16)
- Rnd 4: [3 sc, inc] 4 times. (20)
- Rnds 5-6: Sc evenly around. (20)
- Rnd 7: [4 sc, inc] 4 times. (24)
- Rnd 8: [5 sc, inc] 4 times. (28)
- Rnd 9: [6 sc, inc] 4 times. (32)
- Rnd 10: [7 sc, inc] 4 times. (36)
- Rnds 11-16: Sc evenly around. (36)

Insert safety eyes between Rounds 9 and 10, 7 sts apart. Position eyes so the space between them is on a flat side of the head, giving the squirrel a flat forehead and face.

- Rnd 17: [4 sc, dec] 6 times. (30)
- Rnd 18: [3 sc, dec] 6 times. (24)
- Rnd 19: [2 sc, dec] 6 times. (18)
- Stuff.
- Rnd 20: [sc, dec] 6 times. (12)
- Rnd 21: Dec 6 times. (6)

Bind off leaving long tail for sewing. Thread yarn through remaining 6 sts and pull tight to close.

Attach head to narrow end of body around Round 4, between Rounds 9 and 16 of the head. Center narrow end of head over AC1 side of body.

Ears (Make 2)

- With MC, ch 4.
- Row 1: 8 dc in fourth ch from hook. (see Pattern Notes) (9)

SI st in top of ch-3 to join.

Bind off leaving long tail for sewing.

Sew 2 stitches of ears to head along Round 16, 8 sts apart, aligned with eyes.

Hind Legs (Make 2)

- With MC, ch 2.
- Rnd 1: 6 sc in second ch from hook. (6)
- Rnd 2: Inc in each st around. (12)
- Rnd 3: [sc, inc] 6 times. (18)
- Rnd 4: [2 sc, inc] 6 times. (24)
- Rnd 5: [3 sc, inc] 6 times. (30)
- Rnd 6: [4 sc, inc] 6 times. (36)
- Rnd 7: [5 sc, inc] 6 times. (42)
- Rnds 8-11: Sc evenly around. (42)

Bind off leaving long tail for sewing.

Attach to body between Rounds 9 and 25, equally covering MC and AC1. When leg is sewn ¾ around, stuff, then complete attachment.

Hind Feet (Make 2)

- With AC1, ch 2.
- Rnd 1: 5 sc in second ch from hook. (5)
- Rnd 2: Inc in each st around. (10)
- Rnds 3-8: Sc evenly around. (10)

Bind off leaving long tail for sewing. Stuff lightly. Press last round of Hind Feet flat. Sewing through both layers of the last round, attach across last 4 rounds of hind legs and one round of body. Attach so that first 6 rounds of feet stick out in front of body and act as a stabilizer when body is upright.

Arms (Make 2)

- With AC1, ch 2.
- Rnd 1: 6 sc in second ch from hook. (6)
- Rnd 2: Inc in each st around. (12)
- Rnds 3-4: Sc evenly around. (12)
- Rnd 5: [4 sc, dec] twice. (10)
- Rnds 6: Change to MC, sc evenly around. (10)
- Rnd 7-20: Sc evenly around.

Bind of leaving long tail for sewing. Press paw flat with a slight curve. Holding paw flat, stuff arm. Do not stuff paw. Press last round flat. Working through both layers of the last round, sew arm to body vertically between Rounds 5 and 10, 4 stitches behind the color change. Sew along arm along top and bottom for 4 stitches to tack down and hold pointing forward.

Tail

- With AC2, ch 2.
- Rnd 1: 6 sc in second ch from hook. (6)
- Rnd 2: Inc in each st around. (12)
- Rnd 3: [sc, inc] 6 times. (18)
- Rnd 4: [2 sc, inc] 6 times. (24)
- Rnd 5: [3 sc, inc] 6 times. (30)
- Rnd 6: [4 sc, inc] 6 times. (36)
- Rnd 7: [5 sc, inc] 6 times. (42)
- Rnd 8: [6 sc, inc] 6 times. (48)
- Rnd 9: Skip 24, 24 sc. Leave skipped stitches unworked. (24)
- Rnd 10: Sc evenly around. (24)
- Rnd 11: [2 sc, dec] 6 times. (18)
- Rnd 12: Sc evenly around. (18)
- Rnd 13: [sc, dec] 6 times. (12)
- Rnd 14: Dec 6 times. (6)

Bind off and weave in ends. Continue tail by working on unworked stitches from Round 9.

- Rnd 1: Sc join (see Special Stitches), 23 sc. (24)
- Rnd 2-16: Sc evenly around. (24)

- Rnd 17: [2 sc, dec] 6 times. (18)
- Stuff tail.
- Rnd 18: [sc, dec] 6 times. (12)
- Rnd 19: Dec 6 times. (6)

Bind off, leaving long tail for sewing. Thread yarn through remaining 6 sts and pull tight to close. Sew to body with bottom of tail at Round 22, evenly placed between hind legs, acting as support when body is upright. With scrap yarn, sew center of Round 1 of tail to center of last round of head. Tail will curve along body.

Nose

- With long strand of AC1, sew from the center of the nose, up 2 rounds, and back through center of the nose. Continue in stitches on either side of upper stitch to create a triangle, always threading back through center of nose.

Face Shaping

- Thread yarn up through center of nose and down through stitch 4 rounds straight down from nose. Thread yarn back up through center of nose. Pull tightly to crease snout.

BUTTERFLIES

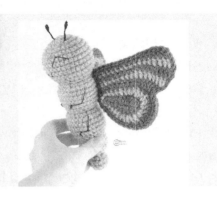

MATERIALS:

- · Lion Brand® WOOL EASE® (Art. #620) – #140 Rose Heather 1 ball (A); #024 Oatmeal 1 ball (B); #114B Denim 1 ball (C)

Lion Brand® crochet hook size F (3.75 mm)
· LION BRAND large-eyed blunt needle

ADDITIONAL MATERIALS: Crochet hook size 1.25 mm; Black Cotton Thread; Fiberfill stuffing
SIZE: About 7 in. (18 cm) tall

ABBREVIATIONS:

- beg = begin(ninig)
- ch = chain
- dc = double crochet
- hdc = half double crochet
- rep = repeat
- rnd(s) = round(s)
- sc = single crochet
- sl st = slip stitch
- st(s) = stitch(es)

BODY

- With A and the bigger hook, make a magic ring.
- Rnd 1: work 8 sc in ring.
- Rnd 2: 2 sc in each st around – 16 sc.
- Rnd 3: * 1 sc, 2 sc in next st; rep from * around – 24 sc.
- Rnd 4: * 2 sc, 2 sc in next st; rep from * around – 32 sc.
- Rnds 5 - 10: sc in each st around.
- Rnd 11: * 2 sc, 2 sc tog; rep from * around – 24 sc.
- Rnd 12: * 1 sc, 2 sc tog; rep from * around – 16 sc.

- Rnd 13: With B, working in front loop, * 1 sc, 2 sc in next st; rep from * around – 24 sc.

Begin stuffing piece and continue stuffing until piece is complete.

- Rnd 14: * 3 sc, 2 sc in next st; rep from * around – 30 sc.
- Rnds 15 - 18: sc in each st around.
- Rnd 19: * 1 sc, 2 sc tog; rep from * around – 20 sc.
- Rnd 20: * 3 sc, 2 sc tog; rep from * around – 16 sc.
- Rnd 21: With A, working in front loop, * 1 sc, 2 sc in next st; rep from * around – 24 sc.
- Rnd 22: * 5 sc, 2 sc in next st; rep from * around – 28 sc.
- Rnds 23 - 25: sc in each st around.
- Rnd 26: * 2 sc, 2 sc tog; rep from * around – 21 sc.
- Rnd 27: * 1 sc, 2 sc tog; rep from * around – 14 sc.
- Rnd 28: With B, working in front loop, * 1 sc, 2 sc in next st; rep from * around – 21 sc.
- Rnds 29 - 31: sc in each st around.
- Rnd 32: * 1 sc, 2 sc tog; rep from * around – 14 sc.
- Rnd 33: 2 sc tog rep around – 7 sc.
- Rnd 34: With A, working in front loop, 2 sc in each st around – 14 sc.
- Rnds 35 - 36: sc in each st around.
- Rnd 37: 2 sc tog rep around – 7 sc.

Fasten off, leaving a long tail. Thread the tail through top of sts of last rnd. Pull tail to close opening and knot securely.

WINGS (make two): With the bigger hook.

Panel I

- Rnd 1: With C, Ch 8, 1 sc in 2nd ch from hook, 1 sc in each of next 2 chs, 1 hdc in next ch, 1 hdc and 1 dc in next ch, 2 dc in next ch, 4 dc in next ch; working along opposite side of beg ch-8, 2 dc in next ch, 1 dc and 1 hdc in next ch, 1 hdc in next ch, 1 sc in each of next 3 chs; join with sl st in first sc – 20 sts.
- Rnd 2: With B, 1 sc in each of next 4 sts, 1 hdc in each of next 2 sts, 2 hdc in next st, 2 dc in next st, 1 dc in next st, 2 dc in each of next 2 sts, 1 dc in next st, 2 dc in next st, 2 hdc in next st, 1 hdc in each of next 2 sts, 1 sc in each of next 4 sts – 26 sts.

- Rnd 3: With C, 1 sc in each of next 9 sts, 2 sc in next st, 1 hdc in next st, 2 dc in each of next 4 sts, 1 hdc in next st, 2 sc in next st, 1 sc in each of next 9 sts – 32 sts.

Start working in back-and-forth rows.

- Row 1: With C, 1 sc in each of next 5 sts, 1 hdc in each of next 3 st, 1 hdc inc in the next st, 2 dc in each of next 3 st; Turn – 16 sts
- Row 2: With A, Ch 2, 2 dc in next st, 1 dc in each of next 5 sts, 1 hdc in each of next 5 sts, 1 sc in each of next 5 sts; Turn – 17 sts.
- Row 3: With C, Ch 1, 1 sc in each of next 10 sts, 1 hdc in each of next 3 st, 1 dc in each of next 3 st, 2 dc in next st; Turn – 18 sts.
- Row 4: With A, Ch 2, dc 2 tog, 1 dc in each of next 3 sts, 1 hdc in each of next 3 sts, 1 sc in each of next 10 sts; Turn – 17 sts.
- Row 5: With C, Ch 1, 1 sc in each of next 10 sts, 1 hdc in each of next 3 st, 1 dc in each of next 2 st, dc 2 tog – 16 sts.

- Fasten off.

Panel II

- Rnd 1: With C, Ch 8, 1 sc in 2nd ch from hook, 1 sc in each of next 2 chs, 1 hdc in next ch, 1 hdc and 1 dc in next ch, 2 dc in next ch, 4 dc in next ch; working along opposite side of beg ch-8, 2 dc in next ch, 1 dc and 1 hdc in next ch, 1 hdc in next ch, 1 sc in each of next 3 chs; join with sl st in first sc – 20 sts.
- Rnd 2: With B, 1 sc in each of next 4 sts, 1 hdc in each of next 2 sts, 2 hdc in next st, 2 dc in next st, 1 dc in next st, 2 dc in each of next 2 sts, 1 dc in next st, 2 dc in next st, 2 hdc in next st, 1 hdc in each of next 2 sts, 1 sc in each of next 4 sts – 26 sts.
- Rnd 3: With C, 1 sc in each of next 9 sts, 2 sc in next st, 1 hdc in next st, 2 dc in each of next 4 sts, 1 hdc in next st, 2 sc in next st, 1 sc in each of next 9 sts; Turn – 32 sts.

Start working in back-and-forth rows.

- Row 1: Facing the back of the wing, With C, 1 sc in each of next 5 sts, 1 hdc in each of next 3 st, 1 hdc inc in the next st, 2 dc in each of next 3 st; Turn – 16 sts.
- Row 2: With A, Ch 2, 2 dc in next st, 1 dc in each of next 5 sts, 1 hdc in each of next 5 sts, 1 sc in each of next 5 sts; Turn – 17 sts.
- Row 3: With C, Ch 1, 1 sc in each of next 10 sts, 1 hdc in each of next 3 st, 1 dc in each of next 3 st, 2 dc in next st; Turn – 18 sts.
- Row 4: With A, Ch 2, dc 2 tog, 1 dc in each of next 3 sts, 1 hdc in each of next 3 sts, 1 sc in each of next 10 sts; Turn – 17 sts.
- Row 5: With C, Ch 1, 1 sc in each of next 10 sts, 1 hdc in each of next 3 st, 1 dc in each of next 2 st, dc 2 tog – 16 sts.
- Do not fasten off.
- Line up edges of Panels I and II, and sl st around through both layers. Fasten off.
- With C, sew Wings to the back of Body, between Rnds 12 and 19, 6 sts apart.
- With Black Cotton Thread, embroider Eyes between Rnds 5 and 8, 4 sts apart.
- With Black Cotton Thread, embroider 2 Arms between Rnds 14 and 19, and 2 Arms between Rnds 21 and 26.

ANTENNAE (make 2)
- With Black Cotton Thread and the smaller hook.
- Rnd 1: 6 sc in ring. Close the ring and work 8 chs.
- Fasten off and leave a strand of thread to sew the antennae to Head between Rnd 1 and Rnd 2. Weave in ends.

TURTLES

Materials

- Approx 75g of chenille yarn in two colors
- 4.5mm crochet hook
- Tapestry Needle
- Polyfil or preferred stuffing
- 12mm safety eyes
- Stitch Marker

Abbreviations

- SC- single crochet
- SC INC- single crochet increase
- HDC- Half Double Crochet
- DC- Double Crochet
- TRC- Triple Crochet
- INV DEC- Invisible decrease

INSTRUCTIONS

Fins

- Using Body color, make four
- Round 1: In a magic circle, HDC 8. Slip stitch to the first stitch and chain one.
- Round 2: HDC INC in each around. (16) Slip stitch to the first stitch and chain one.
- Fold the circle in half and HDC twice through both halves in the first touching stitches. HDC together the next 6 stitches. HDC twice in the last one. (10)

Turtle Head: Using green color

- Round 1: In a magic circle, SC 8.
- Round 2: SC INC in each around. (16)
- Round 3: SC in the first, SC INC in the next. Repeat around. (24)

- Round 4-5: SC in each around. (24)
- Round 6: SC in first, INV DEC in the next. (16)
- Attach the safety eyes between rows 4 and 5, 7 stitches apart.
- Round 7: INV DEC in each around. (8)
- Round 8: SC in each around. (8)
- Fasten off and weave the end in.

Body

- Start with the shell color:
- Round 1: In a magic circle, SC 8.
- Round 2: SC INC in each around. (16)
- Round 3: SC in the first, SC INC in the next. Repeat around. (24)
- Round 4: SC in the first two stitches, SC INC in the next. Repeat around. (32)
- Rounds 5-7: SC in each around. (32)
- Round 8: In the front loop only SC in each around. (32) Change to body color here.
- Round 9:
- In the back loop only, SC in the next two. Attach the first fin through the next two stitches. SC in the next 7. Attach the second fin in the next two stitches. SC in the next. Attach the head going through the next 4 stitches using slip stitches. SC in the next. Attach the third fin stitches in the next two. SC in the next 7. Attach the fin in the next two. Finish the round with the last two sc.
- Round 10: SC in the first 14. Attach the bottom half of the turtles neck with a SC in the remaining 4 stitches. SC in the remaining 14 stitches.
- Round 11: SC in the first two, INV DEC in the next. Repeat around. (24)

- Begin to stuff here. Before you stuff the body, make sure the head and neck have enough stuffing. Continue to stuff as you close.
- Round 12: SC in the first, INV DEC in the next. Repeat around. (16)
- Round 13: INV DEC in each around. (8)
- Sew the remaining hole closed. Fasten off and weave in the ends.

Notes on Attaching the Fins

- The line from the HDCs faces towards the back of the turtle, like this.
- Flip the fin up so that the top now touches the shell. You will be attaching in the two circled stitches.
- On the right side you attach the second to last stitch first. On the left you attach the stitch at the very end of the fin, and then the second.
- Go through the fin and then through the shell. SC as you normally would.
- Repeat through the second stitch.
- This is what it should look like when you are done. The SC should be under the fin.

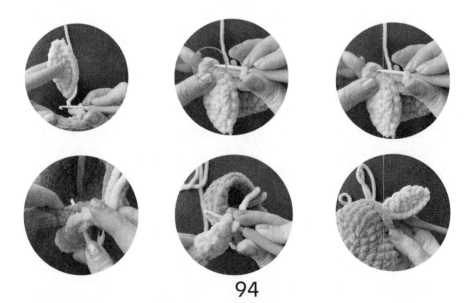

Notes on Attaching the Head

- When you attach the head on row 9, you are only going through 4 of the 8 stitches of the turtle's neck. To find these stitches, flatten the opening so that it is level with the eyes. The top four stitches, when attached, should have the eyes level and on top. For the top stitches you will use slip stitches to attach it to the body. Put your hook through the first stitch on the turtle and then through the corresponding stitch on the body. Pull up and through. You will repeat that three more times for a total of four.

- You will attach the bottom half of the head on the next row. This time you will SC in each of the four bottom stitches across, just like it was a normal part of the row. This leaves a small opening. Make sure you stuff the neck and head pretty well.

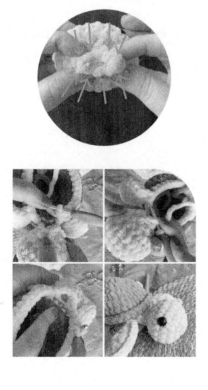

FLAMINGO

Materials and tools:

1. Yarn

- The main color - pink or any other shade of pink color.
- For example, Alize Cotton Gold Nº33 - bright pink, Yarn Art Jeans Nº65 - dusty pink, Nº42
- - fuchsia, Nº61 - bright coral. You can also crochet a bird with a milk color - Alize Cotton
- Gold Nº1.

For the body and head we need approx. 50 g.

For the crocheted wings - approx. 22 g.

For the legs Alize Cotton Gold Nº161- pale pink or Nº67 - milk beige.

For the beak Yarn Art Jeans Nº27 - black and milk or pale pink from the above-listed colors.

2. The hook 2 mm.

3. Stuffing (hollofayber)

4. Two black halfbeads or the safety eyes 10 mm in diameter.

5. A gobelin needle with a big eye.

6 A thin needle with a small eye and a white sewing thread.

7. A moment glue.

8. Fatin - a cut approx. 1 x 1.5 m.

9. A single-strand isolated cable. The diameter of the core is 2 mm. Or any other resilient wire.

10. Cardboard.

Abbreviations

- st - stitch;
- ch-chain;
- Sc single crochet;

96

- inc - increase (crochet 2 sc in one stitch);
- dec decrease (crochet 2 sc together);
- inc3 (crochet 3 sc in one stitch);
- dec3(crochet 3 sc together);
- hdc - half double crochet;
- dc - double crochet;
- sl st slip stitch;
- (sc, inc) x n - repeat those in brackets n-times.
- The size of the ready bird while sitting 22-24 cm.
- All the details except the wings are crocheted in a spiral.
- The crochet pattern contains two variants of making the wings - crocheted wings and wings from the fatin. So, let's start!

HEAD AND BODY

Black color. Stuff in the course of crocheting, not very tight.
- 1 rnd: 6 sc in the magic ring
- 2 rnd: (sc, inc) x 3 (9)
- 3 rnd: 1 sc in each st around (9)
- 4 rnd: (2 sc, inc) x 3 (12)
- 5-6 rnd: 2 rows - 1 sc in each st around (12)
- 7 rnd: (3 sc, inc) x 3 (15)
- 8 rnd: 1 sc in each st around (15)
- 9 rnd: 2 inc, 3 sc, 3 dec, 3 sc, inc (15)
- 10 rnd: 2 sc, inc, 4 sc, dec3, 4 sc, inc (15)
- Further with a milk color
- 11 rnd: (4 sc, inc) x 3 (18)
- 12 rnd: (5 sc, inc) x 3 (21)
- 13-14 rnd: 2 rows - 1 sc in each st around (21)
- 15 rnd: (6 sc, inc) x 3 (24)
- 16 rnd: 1 sc in each st around (24)
- Further with a pink color
- 17 rnd: (3 sc, inc) x6 (30)
- 18 rnd: 1 sc in each st around (30)
- 19 rnd: (4 sc, inc) x 6 (36)
- 20 rnd: 1 sc in each st around (36)

21 rnd: (5 sc, inc) x 6 (42)
22-29 rnd: 8 rows - 1 sc in each st around (42)

Insert the safety eyes: find in the 9th row the middle of three decreases and mark it with a pin. Insert the eyes between the 19 and 20 rows - at the equal space from the center to the sides (pins). The space between the eyes - 15 stitches.

- 30 rnd: (5 sc, dec) x 6 (36)
- 31 rnd: (4 sc, dec) x 6 (30)
- 32 rnd: 1 sc, 3 inc, 7 sc, 6 dec, 7 sc (27)
- 33 rnd: 1 sc in each st around (27)
- 34 rnd: 14 sc, 3 dec, 7 sc (24)
- 35 rnd: 3 sc, inc3, 10 sc, dec3, 7 sc (24)
- 36 rnd: 4 sc, inc3, 10 sc, dec3, 6 sc (24)
- 37 rnd: 5 sc, irc3, 10 sc, dec3, 5 sc (24)
- 38 rnd: 6 sc, inc3, 10 sc, dec3, 4 sc (24)
- 39 rnd: 7 sc, irc3, 10 sc, dec3, 3 sc (24)
- 40 rnd: 8 sc, inc3, 10 sc, dec3, 2 sc (24)
- 41 rnd: 9 sc, inc3, 10 sc, dec3, 1 sc (24)
- 42 rnd: 10 sc, irc3, 10 sc, dec3 (24)
- 43-64 rnd: 22 rows - 11 sc, inc3, 10 sc, dec3 (Crochet a decrease, grasping two last stitches of the current row and the first stitch of the next row. Thus, in each row the beginning of the row moves for one stitch forward)

Advice: flamingo has a thin and graceful neck, that's why do not stuff the neck very tight, do not allow stretching of the cloth. And at the same time the tight stuffing can disturb a wire, which we will later insert inside the neck.

- 65 rnd: 3 inc, 8 sc, inc3, 9 sc, 3 inc (32)
- 66 rnd: (3 sc, inc) x 8 (40)
- 67 rnd: (4 sc, inc) x 8 (48)
- 68 rnd: (7 sc, inc) x 6 (54)
- 69 rnd: (8 sc, inc) x 6 (60)
- 70 rnd: 1 sc in each st around (60)
- 71 rnd: (9 sc, inc) x 6 (66)
- 72 rnd: (10 sc, inc) x 6 (72)
- 73-84 rnd: 12 rows - 1 sc in each st around (72)
- 85 rnd: (10 sc, dec) x 6 (66)
- 86-88 rnd: 3 rows - 1 sc in each st around (66)
- 89 rnd: (9 sc, dec) x 6 (60)
- 90 rnd: 18 sc, 12 dec, 18 sc (48)

Take a wire and bend one end. Fix it with a paper sticky tape.

Insert the wire inside the bird. Push the wire through the stuffing in the body, neck and head by the bent end forward till the black beak. Try to insert in the center, so as the stuffing turned to be around it.

Advice: you can use a wire of a less diameter, but double twisted. If you use an uninsulated wire, you can wind it with a paper sticky tape along the whole length, so it will not slide inside the toy.

- 91-99 rnd: 9 rows - 1 sc in each st around(48)
- 100 rnd: 12 sc, 12 dec, 12 sc (36)
- 101-102 rnd: 2 rows - 1 sc in each st around (36)
- 103 rnd: (4 sc, dec) x 6 (30)
- 104-105 rnd: 2 rows - 1 sc in each st around (30)
- 106 rnd: (3 sc, dec) x 6 (24)
- 107 rnd: 1 sc in each st around (24)
- 108 rnd: (2 sc, dec) x 6 (18)
- 109 rnd: 1 sc in each st around (18)
- 110 rnd: (1 sc, dec) x 6 (12)

Close the opening, tightening the loops.

LEGS (2 pcs)

Pale pink or beige color. Stuff in the course of crocheting.
Crochet 10 ch.

- 1 rnd: beginning from the 2nd loop from the hook
- inc, 7 sc, 4 sc in 1, 3 sc, 2 hdc in 1, 3 sc, inc (23)
- 2 rnd: 12 sc, 1 hdc, 3 sc, dec, 3 sc, 1 hdc, 1 sc (22)
- 3-4 rnd: 12 sc, 1 hdc, 3 sc, 1 hdc, 3 sc, 1 hdc, 1 sc (22)
- 5 rnd: dec, 7 sc, 2 dec, 3 sc, 1 hdc, 3 sc, dec (18)
- 6-7 rnd: 2 rows - 1 sc in each st around (18)
- 8 rnd: dec, 5 sc, 2 dec, 5 sc, dec (14)
- 9 rnd: 1 sc in each st around (14)
- 10 rnd: 8 sc, 6 sl st (14)
- 11 rnd: 8 sc, 6 sl st (14)
- 12 rnd: dec, 4 sc, dec, 6 sc (12)
- 13-35 rnd: 23 rows - 1 sc in each st around (12)
- 36-37 rnd: 2 rows - 1 hdc in each st around (12)

Advice: move the beginning of the row in the 36th row - begin crocheting hdc from the back, so as the transition will be not visible.

- 38-60 rnd: 23 rows - 1 sc in each st around (12)

Crochet several more sc, so as the hook appeared to be on the edge. Lay together the edges and crochet the sc, grasping the both edges. Leave enough thread for sewing. Sew the legs at the level of the 80th row of the body.

CROCHETED WINGS

Crochet chain 60 ch + 1 ch

- 1 rnd: 20 sc, 20 hdc, 20 dc, 3 ch, turn the crocheting.
- 2 rnd: (dc, 1 ch, dc)- in each st, 6 ch, turn the crocheting

- 3 rnd: sc between dc of the previous row. Further alternate 6 ch and sc between dc of the previous row. Crochet this way till the end of the row, evenly increasing the number of ch from 6 till 8 ch.
- Lay together two circles in a spiral.
- Make the third turn an oval one.
- Sew the bases of the circles and a half of an oval.
- Fold the second half of an oval and sew.
- Sew the wings to the body.

FATIN WINGS

Preparing of the fatin:

- Cut out a circle 7 cm in diameter from a cardboard.
- Cut a stripe of fatin of an optional length and 10 cm wide. At the photo the fatin is double folded. Fold this stripe like a roll, so as you can put in a cardboard circle on it.
- Cut out the circles according to the sample. Prepare approx. 100 pcs for one wing.

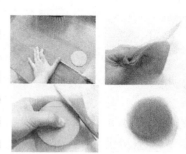

Base for the wing: *Crochet with the main color:*

- 1 rnd: 6 sc in the magic ring
- 2 rnd: 6 inc (12)
- 3 rnd: (sc, inc) x 6 (18)
- 4 rnd: (2 sc, inc) x 6 (24)
- 5 rnd: (3 sc, inc) x 6 (30)
- 6 rnd: (4 sc, inc) x 6 (36)
- 7 row: (5 sc, inc) x 6 (42)
- 8 rnd: not cutting the yarn crochet 7 sc, crochet ch and turn the crocheting
- 9 rnd: 7 sc, ch, turn the crocheting
- 10 rnd: dec, 3 sc, dec, ch, turn the crocheting
- 11 rnd: 5 sc, ch, turn the crocheting
- 12 rnd: dec, 1 sc, dec, ch, turn the crocheting
- 13 rnd: 3 sc

Fasten off and cut the yarn.

Attaching of the fatin:

- Fold a piece of fatin in half three times.
- Insert the hook in the center of the base of the wing. Hitch up the tip of fatin and take itout to the wrong side
- Fasten off this tip with several stitches.

- Attach the fatin this way over each 2 stitches, move along a spiral (from the center to theedge). Attach in rows to a triangle projection

- Sew the wings to the body. Straighten the fatin, pulling for the opposite edge of eachcircle
- It is left only to embroider the eyelashes and your birdy is ready!

104

LIZARDS

Supplies:

- Yarn 4/Medium Weight Yarn in...
- any color
- 4mm Crochet Hook
- .7mm Safety Eyes
- →Tapestry needle
- →Scissors

Head/Body/Tail: In any color

- The head, body, and tail are worked in one continuous piece. We will start with the head.
- Note: You can make this a no-sew lizard if you make the arms/legs first, then simply crochet the leg and body together for 1
- stitch while crocheting the body. I recommend connecting the arms on Round 16. Connect the legs on Round 33. Space the legs out about 5 stitches apart.
- Round 1: 6 Sc into a Magic Ring (6)
- Round 2: *Inc, Sc in the next st* all around (9)
- Round 3: *Sc* all around (9)
- Round 4: *Inc, Sc in the next 2 st* all around (12)
- Round 5: *Inc, Sc in the next 3 st* all around (15)
- Now we will mark where to place the safety eyes. Add a differently colored stitch marker into the 5th and 11th stitch in Round
- 5. Later we will replace the markers with safety eyes.
- Round 6: *Inc, Sc in the next 4 st* all around (18)
- Round 7-9: *Sc* all around (18)
- Round 10: *Dec, Sc in the next st* all around (12)
- Round 11: *Sc* all around (12)
- Place the safety eyes in the marked areas now.

- Round 12: *Dec, Sc in the next 2 st* all around (9)
- Round 13: *Inc, Sc in the next 2 st* all around (12)
- Round 14: *Inc, Sc in the next 3 st* all around (15)
- Round 15: *Inc, Sc in the next 4 st* all around (18)
- Round 16: *Inc, Sc in the next 5 st* all around (21)
- Stuff the head here.
- Round 17: *Inc, Sc in the next 6 st* all around (24)
- Round 18-25: *Sc* all around (24)
- Round 26: *Dec, Sc in the next 2 st* all around (18)
- Stuff here. Continue stuffing after every few rounds.
- Round 27: *Dec, Sc in the next st* all around (12)
- Round 28-30: *Sc* all around (12)
- Round 31: *Dec, Sc in the next 2 st* all around (9)
- Round 32-33: *Sc* all around (9)
- Round 34: *Dec, Sc in the next st* all around (6)
- Round 35: *Sc* all around (6)
- Finish off now, leaving a long tail for sewing. Sew the remaining stitches together. Once done, weave in ends and cut any excess yarn.
- Row 1: Ch 10 . SlSt in the 2nd Ch from the hook. SlSt in the next 3 ch. This forms the first finger.
- Repeat *Ch 4. SlSt in the 2nd Ch from the hook. SlSt in the next 3 ch. SlSt into the same st where the first finger is (Pic 5-6).* 2
- times. Working back on the arm, Sc in the next 5 ch . Finish off, leaving a long tail for sewing. Pin the arms/legs on as
- shown and sew/hot glue on. Once done, weave in ends and cut any excess yarn.

- Finish off, leaving a long tail for sewing. Pin the arms/legs on as shown and sew/hot glue on. Once done, weave in ends and cut any excess yarn.

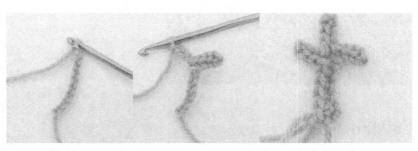

Face Shaping: In any color

- Insert the needle into the bottom of the toy's face as shown. Pull the needle out at the right side of the toy's right eye as shown

- Reinsert needle a few stitches to the left as shown . Pull needle out at the lower face area of the toy

- Reinsert needle one stitch over. Pull needle out at the right side of the toy's left eye
- Reinsert needle a few stitches to the left . Pull needle out at the same stitch where the tail of yarn is coming out
- Pull both ends of yarn to form the face shaping . Now tie both ends of yarn into a firm knot. Bring the knot inside the toy
- to hide, cutting any excess yarn.

107

TIGERS

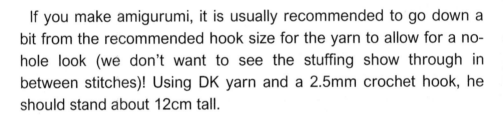

Materials

– A Crochet hook, 2.5mm
– Orange, brown and white DK yarn
– A tapestry needle and scissors
– Stuffing
– Safety eyes and nose (I used 9mm)
– A stitch marker to help you keep track of the start of the round

If you make amigurumi, it is usually recommended to go down a bit from the recommended hook size for the yarn to allow for a no-hole look (we don't want to see the stuffing show through in between stitches)! Using DK yarn and a 2.5mm crochet hook, he should stand about 12cm tall.

Stitches & Abbreviations

The pattern is written using US crochet terms in continuous spirals. You will need to know the following kinds of stitches to make him:
– Magic Ring (MR)
– Single crochet (sc)
– Decrease (dec); preferably using the invisible decrease method
– Increase (inc)
– Changing colors
And now, let's get started!

Head

- Round 1: Starting with orange, 6 sc into a Magic Ring
- Round 2: Inc around (12)
- Round 3: (Sc, inc) around (18)
- Round 4: (Sc 2, inc) around (24)

- Round 5: Sc 3, inc, changing color to brown on the 2nd stitch of the increase, Sc 3, inc, changing color back to orange on the 2nd stitch of the increase, (sc, inc) 4 more times (30)
- Round 6: Sc around (30)
- Round 7: Sc 3, change to brown, sc 9, change to orange, sc 18 (30)
- Round 8-10 (3 rounds): Sc around (30)
- Round 11: Sc 28, change to brown, sc 2 (30)
- Round 12: Sc 5, change to orange, sc 10, change to brown, sc 7, change to orange, sc 8 (30)
- Round 13: Sc 28, change to brown, sc 2 (brown)
- Round 14: Sc 7, change to orange, sc 8, change to brown, sc 9, change to orange, sc 6 (30)
- Round 15: (Sc 4, inc) around (36), insert safety eyes between rounds 11 and 12, 3-4 stitches apart. Start stuffing
- Round 16-17 (2 rounds): Sc around (36)
- Round 18: (Sc 4, dec) around (30)
- Round 19: (Sc 3, dec) around (24)
- Round 20: (Sc 2, dec) around (18), finish stuffing
- Round 21: (Sc, dec) around (12)
- Round 22: Dec around (6), fasten off and close

Body

- Round 1: Starting with orange, 6 sc into a Magic Ring
- Round 2: Inc around (12)
- Round 3: (Sc, inc) around (18)
- Round 4: (Sc 2, inc) around (24), change to brown
- Round 5-13 (9 rounds) : Sc around, alternating between one round of brown and 2 rounds of orange (24)
- Round 14: (Sc 2, dec) around (18)
- Round 15: (Sc, dec) around (12), fasten off, leave a tail for sewing

Ears (Make 2)

- Round 1: Starting with brown, 6 sc into a Magic Ring
- Round 2: (Sc, inc) around (9), change to orange
- Round 3: (Sc 2, inc) around (12)
- Round 4: (Sc 3, inc) around (15)
- Round 5: Sc around (15), change to brown
- Round 6: Sc around (15), change to orange
- Round 7: Sc around (15), fasten off, leave a tail for sewing

Arms (Make 2)

- Round 1: Starting with white, 6 sc into a Magic Ring
- Round 2: (Sc, inc) around (9), change to orange
- Round 3-5: Sc around (9), fasten off, leave a tail for sewing

Legs (Make 2)

- Round 1: Starting with white, 6 sc into a Magic Ring
- Round 2: Inc around (12), change to orange
- Round 3-6: Sc around (12), fasten off, leave a tail for sewing

Snout

- Round 1: Using white, 6 sc into a Magic Ring
- Round 2: Inc around (12)
- Round 3: (Sc 3, inc) around (15)
- Round 4-5 (2 rounds total): Sc around (15), fasten off, leave a tail for sewing

Tail

- You can either make the tail in the round using a Magic Ring, or, if you're like me and you hate crocheting long tubes that are only 6sc thick, you can also crochet this flat, chaning and turning at the end of each row, and sew it together at the end. I started with 3 rows of brown, and then I did alternating sections of orange and brown each 2 rows long for a total of ~17 rows.

Assembly

Sew the body to the head. Add a safety nose (or embroider one) onto the snout, then sew the ears and snout (centered right below/between the eyes) onto the head . Sew on the arms, legs and tail to the body. Done!

Printed in Great Britain
by Amazon

28082650R00066